Cambridge Elements

Elements in Religion and Monotheism
edited by
Paul K. Moser
Loyola University Chicago
Chad Meister
*Affiliate Scholar, Ansari Institute for Global Engagement with Religion,
University of Notre Dame*

MONOTHEISM AND PARADISE

Caitlin Smith Gilson
St. Vincent de Paul Regional Seminary

CAMBRIDGE
UNIVERSITY PRESS

Shaftesbury Road, Cambridge CB2 8EA, United Kingdom

One Liberty Plaza, 20th Floor, New York, NY 10006, USA

477 Williamstown Road, Port Melbourne, VIC 3207, Australia

314–321, 3rd Floor, Plot 3, Splendor Forum, Jasola District Centre, New Delhi – 110025, India

103 Penang Road, #05–06/07, Visioncrest Commercial, Singapore 238467

Cambridge University Press is part of Cambridge University Press & Assessment, a department of the University of Cambridge.

We share the University's mission to contribute to society through the pursuit of education, learning and research at the highest international levels of excellence.

www.cambridge.org
Information on this title: www.cambridge.org/9781009496230

DOI: 10.1017/9781009496216

First published 2024

A catalogue record for this publication is available from the British Library

ISBN 978-1-009-49623-0 Hardback
ISBN 978-1-009-49620-9 Paperback
ISSN 2631-3014 (online)
ISSN 2631-3006 (print)

Cambridge University Press & Assessment has no responsibility for the persistence or accuracy of URLs for external or third-party internet websites referred to in this publication and does not guarantee that any content on such websites is, or will remain, accurate or appropriate.

Monotheism and Paradise

Elements in Religion and Monotheism

DOI: 10.1017/9781009496216
First published online: December 2024

Caitlin Smith Gilson
St. Vincent de Paul Regional Seminary
Author for correspondence: Caitlin Smith Gilson, cgilson@uhcno.edu

Abstract: This Element will provide an essential tracing of selected Greek views of the afterlife which engage in dynamic tension with the Christian understanding of Paradise as fulfilled in the Resurrected state. The main three sections in this Element are Ideas of the Afterlife in the Greek Tragedians; Plato: The Difficulty of Paradise; and Holiness and Violence: A Christian View of the Resurrected State. The imposition of justice and the expiation of guilt through suffering are necessary prerequisites to our approach to the relationship between Monotheism and Paradise. Additional discussions will focus on weak theology and of a God not transcendent enough to ensure the desire for Heaven. As such, the sections are organized to isolate and trace this thread.

Keywords: tragedy, death, fate, Christ, immortality

ISBNs: 9781009496230 (HB), 9781009496209 (PB), 9781009496216 (OC)
ISSNs: 2631-3014 (online), 2631-3006 (print)

Contents

1 Organizational Remarks

"Time is a child playing a game of draughts. The kingship is in the hands of a child."

– Heraclitus

This works seeks to lift the veil on the relationship between a monocentric view of the divine and belief in the afterlife. The particular focus is of a paradisal completion – the alleviation of worldly ethical demand and the fulfillment of imperfect earthly justice. Let us note from the outset that there is a *strong* theological impetus at root in monotheism rather than a *weak* theological understanding of divine potency. In a postmodern theological structure advocating God's weakness, what is rejected is precisely the prevailing Western understanding of God as primal efficient and final metaphysical power. The historic monotheistic claim to God's power is vacated; God is without force and does not and cannot intrude on natural events. "The truth of the event does not belong to the order of identificatory knowledge, as if our life's charge were to track down and learn the secret name of some fugitive spirit."[1] Such a view, while not fully explored in this volume, would open the floodgate to the possibility of Paradise at all, whether such a God has the sufficient causation to bring things to bear, to bring them beyond themselves into transcendent completion.[2]

To situate this text, we understand the backdrop of a strong causal-centric God whose transcendence metaphysically assures a Paradisal realm, and its extended possibility for *knowing* persons through the expiation of guilt by divine judgment. This is crucial to our examination of the underlying hope for Paradise in monotheistic systems. In essence, if there is only one all-powerful Being, God, then all causal structures refer in some fashion to the divine singular existence as ordaining order, as the inescapable beginning and end. We see this strong referential structure in Aquinas' demonstrations, for example in the order of efficient causes necessitating a first efficient cause.[3]

---

[1] Caputo, *The Weakness of God*, 304.

[2] Cf. Tillich, *Systematic Theology, Vol. 1*, 205–206: "The arguments for the existence of God neither are arguments nor are they proof of the existence of God. They are expressions of the question of God which is implied in human finitude. This question if their truth; every answer they give is untrue. This is the sense in which theology must deal with these arguments, which are the solid body of any natural theology. It must deprive them of their argumentative character, and it must eliminate the combination of the words 'existence' and 'God.' If this is accomplished, natural theology becomes the elaboration of the question of God; it ceases to be the answer to this question."

[3] Cf. Aquinas, ST I, 2, 3, *resp*: "There is no case known (neither is it, indeed, possible) in which a thing is found to be the efficient cause of itself; for so it would be prior to itself, which is impossible. Now in efficient causes it is not possible to go on to infinity, because in all efficient causes following in order, the first is the cause of the intermediate cause, and the intermediate is the cause of the ultimate cause, whether the intermediate cause be several, or only one. Now to

This tracing of monotheism will focus on the Greco-Christian understanding, from the Pre-Socratics, the Greek tragedians, Plato, to the early Christian inheritors of the Greek worldview. The imposition of justice and the expiation of guilt through suffering are necessary prerequisites to our approach to the relationship between Monotheism and Paradise. As such, the three sections are organized to isolate and trace this thread: Section 2: Ideas of the Afterlife in the Greek Tragedians; Section 3: Plato: The Difficulty of Paradise; Section 4: Holiness and Violence: A Christian View of the Resurrected State.

1.1 Framing Remarks on the Pre-Socratics

There is an interpretative lineage, a growing monotheistic emphasis, in the Pre-Socratics. Here are brief framing remarks so that our turn to the tragedians is informed by these historical influences. Aristotle, for example, gives credit to Thales for being the original thinker to ponder what is the underlying or basic substance of the universe.[4] This direct questioning of primal causation – "the first cause" – of existence by and through which everything else proceeds, is an essential step in influencing the arch of monotheism which wholly characterizes Western civilization. Even Thales' resolution, water, is suggestive. He knew that whatever the First Cause was had to have some degree of emancipatory power to be unified to everything that followed. This is by no means transcendence, but it gives us a glimmer of a unifying principle that must be immanent in all things and survive that immanence, claiming a nascent filiation with transcendent reality. For Thales, water took on various states. It became vapor when heated and solid when frozen, it could be mixed with the earth, and could gain enough pressure to move the earth; it also provided life, central to the growth of living things. It appeared that water enjoyed a privilege amid all the elements and had the highest hierarchical value; thus it must be the unifying element.

Anaximander sensuously and suggestively provided a true metaphysical nuance to the First Cause, and undoubtedly influenced the Christian understanding of God. In his concept of the *apeiron*, this unifying principle was "the unlimited, boundless, infinite, or indefinite."[5] While Thales' water could not claim a *positive* transcendent value needed for a genuine origin to monotheism, the *apeiron* was far more the irreducible mystery, the indefinite ground prefiguring all grounds, the boundless creative force with the capacity to set order,

---

take away the cause is to take away the effect. Therefore, if there be no first cause among efficient causes, there will be no ultimate, nor any intermediate cause. But if in efficient causes it is possible to go on to infinity, there will be no first efficient cause, neither will there be an ultimate effect, nor any intermediate efficient causes; all of which is plainly false. Therefore, it is necessary to admit a first efficient cause, to which everyone gives the name of God."

[4] Aristotle, *Metaphysics*, 983b21.   [5] Anaximander, Baird, *Philosophical Classics*, 10.

structure, and to be at the helm of the creation, destruction, and recreation of new forms: the limitless not-a-thing. The beginnings of the unifying transcendent agent are present in seedling form. For Anaximander, no first cause could be reduced to a natural element. These elements are created, destroyed, and renewed. Something prior and *other* must be at work. In the *Physics,* Aristotle reflects on Anaximander's vision:

> But yet, nor can the infinite body be one and simple, whether it be, as some say, that which is beside the elements, from which they generate the elements, or whether it be expressed simply. For there are some people who make what is beside the elements the infinite substance; for the elements are opposed to each other (for example, air is cold, water moist, and fire hot), and if one of these were infinite the rest would already have been destroyed. But, as it is, they say that the infinite is different from these, and that they come into being from it.[6]

Not being a material element, the *apeiron* is not within the cyclical generation of those things. The boundless is indeterminate and beyond opposition, thus opening the door to the sense of it as impassable and infinite.

Is there a step back taken with Anaximander's student Anaximenes? Did Anaximander make an advance, elevating the primal principle into metaphysical foundation which Anaximenes squanders when he postulates air as the first cause? Perhaps: haven't we gone from a truer comprehensive principle of the boundless no-thing, to a particular that cannot truly raise itself above change? Is this a mere recitation of Thales? But the question for our purposes is what is gained, if anything, in the formation of a monotheism when Anaximenes decides upon air as unifying basic principle of existence. Anaximenes makes an advance over Thales by instituting an explanatory process of observable change. The change, for instance, in the density of air becomes fire. The process of condensation transforms air, and so on. These observable differences to the elements are the product of measurable changes initiating a scientific view. What we may infer is the continued tension between the physical and metaphysical views of existence, as well as the scientific and theological origins. Most critically, the desire to create a bridge within those varying causations that link them, but without sublation and reduction, particularly in a Christian monotheism.

Anaximenes' detailed focus on the quantifiable changes to matter also promotes a worldview of change and flux central to the mystery of a monotheistic God who must be unchanging, eternal, but who causes, as well as endures, otherness and change.[7] We also see a tension in the oft-paired Pre-Socratic

---

[6] Aristotle, *Physics*, 204b22.

[7] For all of Plato's much emphasized preoccupation with the unworldly form, he knew the problematic bifurcation of *stasis* and flux. In a Christian context, it plagues any thought of Paradise. Cf. Plato, *Parmenides*, 141e: "Then if the one has no participation in time whatsoever,

writings of Parmenides who enshrines the unchanging eternal as the path of the True, opposed to the Heraclitean flux which drew Nietzsche into its suggestive orbit for its culture and religious foundations. One question we must have in the interpretive background is whether any monotheism can genuinely endure otherness and change, or does it alienate and create a false path from the outset preferring a stasis in all arenas opposed to vitality?[8] "Heraclitus of Ephesus thought that the nature of things was hidden but discoverable, and he chastised those who failed to discern the unapparent in the apparent. We might expect then that Heraclitus would divulge in some way to the hapless many how wisdom is to be got."[9] But what informs monotheism more, and perhaps problematically, is the Parmenidean view. Parmenides envisioned that nothing changes in reality; our senses convey the perception of change. "We can speak and think only of what exists. And what exists is uncreated and imperishable for it is whole and unchanging and complete. It was not nor shall be different since it is now, all at once, one and continuous."[10] If change is an illusion and the essence of reality unifies every human being, to achieve this true reality entices the person into a transcendent or beyond-world search where stasis *as stasis* is experience. The question remains whether this is the path to Paradise outlined by monotheism, and is it one that endures otherness, change? Heraclitus does not diminish change but sees everything changing in time; famously we "do not step into the same river twice." Forever new waters are always meeting us, and we are changing with them. Such a view lends far more easily to the weak theology of a God not transcendent enough to ensure the expiation of guilt, the demands of justice, or the Paradisal abode available to humanity.

As we continue to scan the land of the Pre-Socratic contributions which lay the groundwork for the architecture of monotheism or, more rarely, reside in tension, as did Heraclitus, we reflect on how this current lends to certain modern predicaments. The offering of transcendent permanence in monotheism, in nascent form in the Parmenidean stasis, always resides in tension with the dynamic overwhelming change of Heraclitean flux. The integrity of the latter dramatically calls into question the possibility of Paradise as a metaphysical

---

it neither has become nor became nor was in the past, it has neither become nor is it becoming nor is it in the present, and it will neither become nor be made to become nor will it be in the future . . . Can it then partake of being in any other way than in the past, present, or future? It cannot. Then the one has no share in being at all . . . Then it has no being even so as to be one, for if it were one, it would be and would partake of being; but apparently one neither is nor is one, if this argument is to be trusted."

[8] Heraclitus, and his great inheritor Nietzsche, evokes the non-way particularity of wisdom as opposed to the dominating unchanging, universalizing Parmenidean way. This non-way appears to be the thread opposing monotheistic currents.

[9] Pritzl, "On the Way to Wisdom in Heraclitus," 305.

[10] Velasquez, *Philosophy: A Text with Readings*, 10.

reality. Additionally, the preference for stasis within the strong theological underpinnings of monotheism, appears to resist newness and societal change, advocating a conservatism of norms and traditional practices which do align with, and augment, the view of a transcendent Paradise. Heraclitus' *panta rhei* – "everything is in flux" – had prophetically substituted "God" with "Change." Existence is the cosmogonic mixing of opposites, the overthrowing of one value for another, the relentless process of destruction and renewal. Change is a violent, seductive, and erotic process of war, strife, power. To accept this reality is wisdom. The historical lineage binding Heraclitus to Nietzsche and into postmodernity involves an allegiance to flux and innovation, which casts its revolution on all facets of society, from ethics to religion, heralding progressivism, and the death of God. While this evokes the resurrection of divine meaning in diverse forms, flux *per se* is too weak for those classic Paradisal promises.

The relational intensity between the demands of permanence and the sheer presence of change, so integral to monotheistic articulations of Paradise, is seen most acutely in the drama of the human soul. The soul that must endure the body and, in some instances – most particularly within Christianity – long for the reunification with that body, so that Paradise, in monotheism, becomes the *only* place where the tensions between stasis and flux are finally resolved, not only in the body, but in justice and redemption. In the Pre-Socratics, we see an inkling of this tension in Pythagoras. For Pythagoras, the perfect symmetry and order of number is the underlying principle of truthful existence. Number calls to mind the step removed from nature which Anaximander's *apeiron* evokes. Mathematical reality has no beginning or ending, it stands apart, preceding the existence of motion and change and all the earthly elements. The soul is viewed as possessing the quality of number, enduring change, and retaining its immortality. The soul for Pythagoras is eternal, passing through a multitude of lives and incarnations, acquiring new knowledge of what it is, in different forms, experienced in diverse ways. This view was a key in forming the Transmigration of Souls which influenced Plato and Neoplatonism, and the underlying predicament of how transcendence relates to immanence. The unresolved issue remains central: how and whether the unchanging divine endures otherness and change, and more radically incorporates this reality in Paradise. This predicament is not only *not* resolved in Pythagoras, but also not resolved in Plato or Aristotle. Its resolution is a critical piece in the puzzle of a comprehensive view of Paradise formed under one God, one which espouses the metaphysics of endurance and permanence yet one carefully attuned to the individual and unrepeatable, the qualities essential to persons in flux. Is the dignity of the individual able to be preserved in a monotheistic view of Paradise where the hegemony of the divine prefers universal and eternal categories?

The Pythagorean soul implies an underlying governing force from which each soul proceeds, and returns to, after death. But it is Xenophanes who fleshes out this elusive set-apart governance. Although Pythagoras brings us to a sense of salvific endurance through truth, still the unifying power is left undefined, the radicality of its transcendence and otherness to all things is not clarified. It is Xenophanes who gives us the monotheistic God, against the many anthropomorphised versions. "There is one god, among gods and men the greatest, not at all like mortals in body or in mind. He sees as a whole, thinks as a whole, and hears as a whole. But without toil, he sets everything in motion by the thought of his mind."[11] Here we see that the origins of monotheism strike at the very heart of the human person and the ratification on a metaphysical level of that Pre-Socratic poetic immortality which raises us above the animals. With Xenophanes we see more clearly that the drama of the human person is at stake in a monotheism which *must* offer Paradisal fulfillment. His primal spiritual Other, clearly irreducible to anything in the world, has the power to set things in motion; its agency as indivisible whole enables this originating process. The fulfilling truth we seek, truth suggestive of Paradisal completion, demands knowledge beyond us, a capacity to experience wholeness beyond us: "The truth is that no man ever was or will be who understands the gods and all I speak of. If you stumble on some rocks of the whole truth you never know it. There is always speculation."[12] Beings are set in motion and proceed along this course through decay, atrophy until death. Xenophanes suggests a reuniting with the creative force, but is it a surrendering, a disengagement, an absence of knowledge on the part of the human who stumbles on earth to know, and more often than not makes gods in his own image? In surviving fragments, Xenophanes clearly is striking at the difference between gods made in man's image versus a creative power *beyond* image.

> Man made his gods, and furnished them with his own body, voice, and garments. If a horse or lion or a slow ox had agile hands for paint and sculpture, the horse would make his god a horse, the ox would sculpt an ox. Our gods have flat noses and black skins say the Ethiopians. The Thracians say our gods have red hair and hazel eyes.[13]

While we have a glimpse of the hegemonic transcendent power which may inhabit a Paradisal abode, we do not have human epistemological participation in it. Our participation is reductive, counterfeit even, made in our image, unable to endure Being *beyond* image, that boundless infinity of the *apeiron*. Can we know Xenophanes' God who is entirely beyond change? God "sees all over, thinks all

---

[11] Xenophanes, Baird, *Philosophical Classics*, 18.
[12] Xenophanes, Baird, *Philosophical Classics*, 19.
[13] Xenophanes, *Early Greek Philosophy*, 43.

Figure 1 Trojan Horse.JPG, by Carol Scott

over, hears all over. He remains always in the same place, without moving; nor is it fitting that he should come and go, first to one place then to another. But without toil he sets all things in motion by the thought of his mind."[14]

2 Ideas of the Afterlife in the Greek Tragedians

"He steered the mortal mind to thought, making one law: suffer and learn. Drop by drop on hearts in sleep falls pain, remembering woes; and so to the unwilling comes wisdom when it comes. Violent is the grace of powers at the terrible helm."
　　　　　　　　　　　　　　　　　　　　　– Aeschylus, *Agamemnon*[15]

"Behold me, princes of Thebes, the last daughter of the house of your kings, see what I suffer, and from whom, because I feared to cast away the fear of Heaven!"
　　　　　　　　　　　　　　　　　　　　　　　– Sophocles, *Antigone*[16]

---

[14]　Xenophanes, Robinson, *An Introduction to Early Greek Philosophy*, 53.
[15]　Aeschylus, *Agamemnon*, 174–79.　　[16]　Sophocles, *Antigone*, 940–43.

This section will address Aeschylus' *Oresteia* and Sophocles' *Oedipus* cycles, particularly focusing on the sufferings of Orestes and Oedipus. In doing so, several intensifying themes will come to bear fruit, particularly on the question of the essence of the tragic in relation to a centralizing divine order.

These cycles place us within the cosmogonic in tension with the transcendent, amid the old gods and the new, of fate in relation to human and divine wills, evoking the coexistence and yet opposition of heaven and earth. Here we arrive at the preliminary tension of the very essence of tragedy that evokes a compact and unexpressed filiation realized in the figure of the God-Man as exemplar of monotheistic expressions. The tragic finally occurs or completes itself when the guiltless become guilty but, at the same time, and because of how the guilt is wrought, subverts the very tragic element. The tragic is not so much death itself, but the torn, violent separation of the body and soul that occurs throughout all human life as both entirely unexpected and utterly unavoidable.

The nascent anthropology of both cycles places us within the demands of the afterlife as united to *dike* and indelibly linked to death. One cannot easily destroy a being who is deemed immortal. The type of suffering in tragedy is the pulling apart and separating of what wholly resists separation. That it occurs even to the guilty involves a degree of guiltlessness – what is transpiring in suffering is irremediably worse than any transgression.

2.1 The *Agamemnon*: Zeus, Knowledge, and Suffering

The opening lines of the Oresteia, in the *Agamemnon*, are grounded in the philosophy of suffering, and expiation wrought through divine power.

> Zeus: whatever he may be, if this name
> pleases him in invocation,
> thus I call upon him.
> I have pondered everything
> yet I cannot find a way,
> only Zeus, to cast this dead weight of ignorance
> finally from out my brain.
> He who in time long ago was great,
> throbbing with gigantic strength,
> shall be as if he never were, unspoken.
> He who followed him has found
> his master, and is gone.
> Cry aloud without fear the victory of Zeus,
> you will not have failed the truth:
> Zeus, who guided men to think,
> who has laid it down that wisdom
> comes alone through suffering.

> Still there drips in sleep against the heart
> grief of memory; against
> our pleasure we are temperate
> From the gods who sit in grandeur
> grace comes somehow violent.[17]

Suffering is the central inescapable reality around which all things – mind, body, spirit, culture, education – orbit. At times, some of these civilizational aspects are pulled unbearably closer so that the human person can hardly endure its violence. Suffering is what separates mortals; it is the crucible throwing lives into mania and madness. The opening lines of the *Agamemnon* are decisive in our tracing of the cohesive monotheism where all promises, doctrines, and hopes are fulfilled in Paradise. The goals of lives are fraught with illusion, deception, lack of clarity, and dwindling promise – truth is what is sorely lacking. In the opening Hymn to Zeus, we see the linking of a hegemonic divine power as Truth. Our salvation from the descent into madness revolves around turning to Zeus who is Truth. The human person has pondered and attempted different avenues to save himself, yet there is no way he can conceive or elicit salvific freedom. Only Zeus can cast out the "dead weight of ignorance" where "grace comes somewhat violent." This is a radical and revolutionary unifying set of themes – one God as Truth, elevating the person out of inescapable suffering and untruth. Zeus as God is not only guarantor of *episteme*, He *is* knowledge. Here we see the planted seed of monotheistic strength and demand – the "pondering" in the opening lines makes it clear that truth is an absolute undiminished reality at which one arrives through grace or fails to witness and experience. Truth is irreducible, inconvertible, transcendent, and Other. The only way one is set free from suffering is *through* the suffering to recover the certain and universal wisdom set down by Zeus. This reality stretches through the *Oresteia* and we see it in the *Eumenides* and in the guardianship of our hearts: "There is a time when fear is good and ought to remain seated as a guardian of the heart. It is profitable to learn wisdom under strain."[18] This strain and stretching forth of the heart conjures a hierarchical goal – one where the just man is never "utterly destroyed," while at the one who transgresses, "the god laughs."

I have a timely word of advice: arrogance is truly the child of impiety, but from health of soul comes happiness, dear to all, much prayed for . . . Whoever is just willingly and without compulsion will not lack happiness; he will never be utterly destroyed. But I say that the man who boldly transgresses, amassing a great heap unjustly – by force, in time, he will strike his sail, when trouble seizes him as the yardarm is splintered. He calls on those who hear nothing and

---

[17] Aeschylus, *Agamemnon*, 160–83.   [18] Aeschylus, *Eumenides*, 517.

he struggles in the midst of the whirling waters. The god laughs at the hot-headed man, seeing him, who boasted that this would never happen, exhausted by distress without remedy and unable to surmount the cresting wave. He wrecks the happiness of his earlier life on the reef of Justice, and he perishes unwept, unseen.[19]

The healthy soul is salvific and is cultivated through a transformation of thought, of a recovery of reality from the many appearances. Salvation is not ultimately the product of human enterprise, it is a grace aligned with justice (*dike*) through the hegemony of Zeus *as* incontrovertible, absolute truth. The Hymn affirms the *arche* and *telos* within human epistemology, making an advance in Greek thought: the human person must turn to the originating, guiding, and ending principle of all things, this *periagoge* is essential to overcome pain and to orient human nature. The human person cannot *be* truly his own without stabilizing divine reality which casts away madness. The two poles of *episteme* and madness and the drama of the human turn (*periagoge*) in-between give us a very preliminary spiritual psychology of Paradise and its alternative, Hell. Heaven as identical with Truth, and the loss of the divine as madness, the whirling disintegration of person, truth, and being we understand to be Hell. Why? Because Aeschylus, not in compact mystical utterance, but in clear expression has set down the rules of existential reality. The knowledge of truth, entering union with Zeus who can hurl madness and ignorance aside, is essential for salvation.

The tension magnifies: knowledge which casts aside madness, also commences madness. Our epistemological gift is the self-same recognition of our mortality, the mortalizing reality that brings anxiety, dread, fear, and suffering. Knowledge strips us and unveils our mortality, and only the higher truest kind of knowledge, given through divine grace as wisdom, can set us free from that suffering. Knowledge reveals becoming and nothingness, and knowledge sets out the passage to immortality and Being. Aeschylus unveils this paradoxical reality of Being and Becoming in an unprecedented manner, one which places us within the ontological question of the soul, and of what survives of the person after death.

The opening lines of the *Agamemnon* transfer us from an awareness of suffering to a fully realized dilemma of ontologically grounded suffering.[20]

---

[19] Aeschylus, *Eumenides*, 527–60.

[20] By ontologically grounded suffering, I mean one which accepts the collision of fate and free will within every life into its bones and sinews. This collision is not overcome nor is life, knowledge, and experience a process of suffering in which we shed its anchor. To undergo life is "to suffer" or to "take on." Suffering is the lasting companion of a human life and it the giver of meaning. Cf. Cioran, *The Trouble with Being Born*, 10: "People have not understood that suffering is the only means of fighting against mediocrity. We cannot change too much by means of culture or spirit;

This is the move that makes the drama of the afterlife in monotheism so critical. The beckoning of Zeus to save is prompted by unbearable knowledge, by the ontological acknowledgment of the absolute either/or: transcendence or annihilation, immortality or totalizing nothingness, life as true endurance or death as unrecoverable dissolution. Aeschylus' elucidation of this dilemma invites a more extreme and realized form of suffering. Ontologically realized suffering changes the outlook and trajectory of life and necessitates the imposition of justice on a divine level.[21] We see this ontological either/or in the *Suppliant Women*. It is an all or nothing, and human anthropology is bound up wholly in the outcome. Will the heart remain "unexercised in tears"? Are there "any friendly kinsman here to champion our band which has fled from the haze-shrouded land."[22]

> Zeus' desire is hard to trace: it shines everywhere, even in gloom, together with fortune obscure to mortal me. Safely it falls, and not upon its back, whatever deed comes to pass at Zeus' nod; for the pathways of his understanding stretch dark and tangled, beyond comprehension. From their high-towering hopes he hurls mankind to utter destruction; yet he does not marshal any armed violence – all that is wrought by the powers divine is free from toil. Seated on his holy throne, unmoved, in mysterious ways he accomplishes his will . . . Sacrifices in satisfaction of vows are given freely to the gods when all fares well, if only there be escape from death. Alas, alas, perplexing troubles! Where will this wave of trouble bear me away?[23]

In essence, Aeschylus leaves no doubt of the dilemma of human nature. Either death is an annihilating finality which nothing survives, or Zeus as transcendent Other has the power to recover us, but his ways are beyond us, "the pathways of his understanding stretch dark and tangled, beyond comprehension." The hope in Zeus, this existential wager, is at the core of monotheism's power. The strong historical movement of the hegemonic reality to outwit and to overcome the nothingness of death, to overcome the madness and anxiety that it prompts, is achieved through wisdom irreducible to worldly or human powers. For this to be possible – for us to be liberated from the nothingness we are being drawn toward with disease, age, and dying, humans must possess an

---

but it is unimaginable how much we can change through pain. The only weapon against mediocrity is suffering."

[21] Cf. von Balthasar, *You Crown the Year with Your Goodness*, 89: "When what is required of us seems too burdensome, when the pains become unbearable and the fate we are asked to accept seems simply meaningless – then we have come very close to the man nailed on the Cross at the Place of the Skull, for he has already undergone this on our behalf and, moreover, in unimaginable intensity."

[22] Aeschylus, *The Suppliants*, 68–72. [23] Aeschylus, *The Suppliants*, 87–127.

irreducible essence that is forever immune to death, and is the epistemological companion to transcendental truth.

The *Oresteia* also presents us with structure of fate, imperfect justice, and the radical need for a divine foundation that can impose order and justice. As we well know, Trojan prince Paris runs off with Helen. Menelaus, Helen's husband, is irate and his brother, Agamemnon, a distinguished and important Greek statesman is now compelled to punish this affront against his family, to restore justice, by leading an army into Troy. But the goddess Artemis is supportive of the Trojans and prevents Agamemnon's army from sailing across the Aegean. Agamemnon is faced with an impossible choice, two alternatives which cannot escape failure of duty. Either Agamemnon relinquishes the demands of duty and gives up the expedition to Troy, thereby failing to honor his brother, the king, or he pleases Artemis by sacrificing his daughter Iphigenia, thereby failing in his duty as a father. While Agamemnon chooses freely and choses the latter both fates bind him and he is in its inescapable netting.

> And her father told his servants after a prayer
> to lift her face downwards like a goat above the altar,
> as she fell about his robes to implore him with all her heart,
> and by gagging her lovely mouth
> to stifle a cry
> that would have brought a curse upon his house;
> using violence, and the bridle's stifling power.
> And with her robe of saffron dye streaming downwards
> she shot each of the sacrificers
> with a piteous dart from her eye,
> standing out as in a picture, wishing
> to address each by name, since often
> in her father's hospitable halls
> she had sung, and virginal with pure voice
> had lovingly honored the paean
> of felicity at the third libation of her loving father.[24]

This awful sacrifice allowed the Greeks to reach Troy and claim victory, but it destroyed Agamemnon's wife Clytemnestra, who is filled with seething, blinding rage. During Agamemnon's absence, Clytemnestra commences an affair with his cousin Aegisthus and, upon Agamemnon's return, she and Aegisthus savagely kill him in the bath, entangling him in a cloth net and stabbing him as he is trapped in the web bleeding out.[25] But the cycle of vengeance continues

---

[24] Aeschylus, *Agamemnon*, 231–48.

[25] In the figure of Clytemnestra, we have a key foreshadowing of the expiation of guilt through suffering. Clytemnestra accepts responsibility for being the architect of Agamemnon's murder through the belief that human beings are the total bearers of justice, and all that it imposes:

with Orestes, the son of Agamemnon and Clytemnestra. He avenges his father by killing his own mother. The problematic expiation of guilt and the imperfect role of justice are central to the *Oresteia* trilogy:

> The whole house has been wrong since the quarrel of Atreus and Thyestes. Atreus was hideous in murder, but this does not justify Aegisthus in murdering Agamemnon, any more than the sins of Agamemnon justified his murder by Clytemnestra, or the sins of Paris and Helen justified the obliteration of Troy. All the executioners plead that they act for just retribution, but the chain of murder has got out of hand and is perpetuating itself, until it seems no longer to come from personal purpose but has grown into a Curse, a Thing. Every correction is a blood-bath which calls for new correction.[26]

In the *Oresteia*, when one act of violence occurs, it inevitably threatens to set off a chain reaction of endless retaliatory violence and interminable rectifying vengeance. Revenge here isn't solely retaliatory but also seeks to reform/ teach the offender justice through a sheer experience of how his original offense was unjust. Vengeance is viewed as the punishment designed to express how much human beings abhor violence, but once within vengeance, the cycle cannot be broken without sacrifice which unites enemies in a common cause, in a common enemy to be sacrificed which alleviates their anger, tensions, and desires for vengeance. But this redemptive violence can never truly redeem. Such an act cannot escape that cycle of fatalist violence for no act of redemptive violence is permanent. Aeschylus is setting up the very architectonic of monotheistic power and need. There must a divine force strong enough to extol justice, to balance the scales. There are gods such as Artemis who insinuate themselves changing the course of human action, and there is the Godhead, more transcendent and other, which must somehow – *per impossibile* – set everything right. History has always been on the hunt for a tangible, fleshy expiation of our guilt through suffering.[27]

Justice within the *Agamemnon* is an imperfect, violent, self-perpetuating system of historical family murder. The next two plays attempt to reconcile this self-perpetuating violence, to stop the domino effect of fated retribution. In the second play, the *Libation Bearers*, the chorus states, "It is the law: when the

---

punishment as well as lengths of seen and unseen consequences. At the close of the *Agamemnon*, she willingly accepts her fate in suffering the consequences, yet begs her lover and co-conspirator Aegisthus that there be no more grief, that the cycle end, but acknowledges that their lives, due to their choices, are now linked to pain and suffering. Clytemnestra knows she cannot escape the poisoned fruits of her actions and resigns herself as both victor and loser and through this illuminates a starting point for atonement, that is, making oneself one with truth and fate.

[26] Lattimore, *The Proper Study*, 63.

[27] Cf. Lev. 17:11: "For the life of the flesh is in the blood, and I have given it for you on the altar to make atonement for your souls, for it is the blood that makes atonement by the life."

blood of slaughter wets the ground it wants more blood. Slaughter cries for the Fury of those long dead to bring destruction on destruction churning in its wake!"[28] Apollo has encouraged and sanctioned Orestes' matricide. The god has attempted to quell the blood feud by this form of divine justice, still Orestes is not fully emancipated from the cycle of guilt. And Apollo's divine sanction does not equal divine justice.

> He died
> without honor when he came home. It was my mother of the dark heart, who . . .
> cut him down.
> The bath is witness to his death.
> I was an exile in the time before this. I came back
> and killed the woman who gave me birth. I plead guilty.
> My father was dear, and this was vengeance for his blood.
> Apollo shares responsibility for this.
> He counterspurred my heart and told me of pains to come
> if I should fail to act against the guilty ones.[29]

In the *Eumenides*, a legal system is then formed to overcome revenge killing – to banish the furies – and to offer something other than expiation by blood feud, a system which declares Orestes innocent. But is he truly innocent? In this whole process of burgeoning justice, we see the once immanentized divinity being remodeled into a system attempting to accommodate the demands of higher ordered justice, a demand that when fully fleshed out, as we will see, necessitates paradisal dimension. The Fates and Justice are not mere abstracted concepts for the Greeks, they are ordained by Zeus, by the godhead who alone can elevate us out of madness. To depart from Justice is not merely to violate an abstract concept, but to offend a deity itself. This conceptual move is crucial to a monotheistic understanding of Paradise.[30]

There shall be peace forever between these people . . .

> Zeus the all seeing
> met with Destiny to confirm it.
> Singing all follow our footsteps.[31]

2.2 *Oedipus Rex*: Fate and Free Will

Here we turn to Sophocles' *Oedipus Rex* and the underlying philosophical themes of fate and freedom in the *agon* of human choice. This collision between

---

[28] Aeschylus, *Libation Bearers*, 420–23.   [29] Aeschylus, *Eumenides*, 458–67.

[30] Cf. Heb. 9:22: "Indeed, under the law almost everything is purified with blood, and without the shedding of blood there is no forgiveness of sins."

[31] Aeschylus, *Eumenides*, 1040–47.

a predestined arch and human free will which comes to a climax for Oedipus, mirrors and influences the heights of the Christian theo-drama. The radicality of the Christ event, the Crucifixion, marries fate and freedom to the point of death, and is essential to the human reception of Paradise given by God. Christ is paradoxically the only human being born intended to die, and as fully God He is the only Being Who can overcome death. The underlying spiritual violence, the quaking reverberations through history, that the reality of free will in no way opposes fate, is at the depth of *Oedipus Rex*. It is essential to examine the tragedy to see how its themes foreshadow the demands of a singular God as the ordaining, bringing, and completing force of human action as both entirely free *and* already given. The ultimacy of free choice means that judgment – Heaven, Hell, Purgatory – are the fair conclusions of a human life, while the already given fate assures that the central power of God is a strong theology, a One God Whose transcendence can fulfill judgment and the commission of Paradise.[32]

> But now whose tale is more painful to hear?
> who dwells with disasters, with pangs
> more savage than your shifting life?
> io, glorious Oedipus!
> For the same wide
> Harbor lay open
> as son and husband
> fathering children – how,
> how could the furrow
> sown by your father
> bear you in silence so long?[33]

The story of Oedipus in different forms is found through Ancient Greece, from Homer, Hesiod and Pindar. Only fragments remain of Euripides' own *Oedipus* tragedy. The most famous version comes from Sophocles' Theban cycle of plays: *Oedipus Rex, Oedipus at Colonus, and Antigone*. Aristotle in the *Poetics* considered the story of Oedipus the most perfect tragedy, issuing in the audience the dramatic variety of *pathos* of genuine human experience. We can see the beginnings of dealing with the tension of fate and free will in Aristotle's remarks on the relationship of a human situation to probability:

---

[32] Again, we see this strong emphasis on transcendence opposed to the deconstructive situation of a weak theology which places the weight on human action within an immanent finite boundary that is never transgressed. Cf. Caputo, *Religion with/out Religion*, 164: "Religious faith, I would say, is an instantiation of a deconstructive situation in which we are asked to affirm, to make an act of faith, and to make an act of faith which is motivated by love, by the love of justice and what is to come, that mourns for the dead, that hopes for the future . . . It [deconstruction] has not come into the world to tell humankind what to do. It is a kind of salutary description of the conditions under which we act, but that is all."

[33] Sophocles, *Oedipus Rex*, 1205–16.

The poet should prefer for his situations impossibilities which are probable rather than possibilities which are improbable. On the other hand, he should not compose stories of irrational elements. While it is best for a play to have nothing irrational, if it does, it should be outside the actions of the play, like Oedipus not knowing how Laius died.[34]

In the tragedy, Oedipus was the son of King Laius and Queen Jocasta of Thebes. They were childless for a long time and because of this and the surprise of the pregnancy, King Laius consulted the Oracle of Apollo at Delphi as to his future in relation to the child. The Oracle prophesied that any son born to the king would kill him. Jocasta naturally bore a son, prompting Laius to use all power and free will to outwit the prophesy, yet his very actions play into the underlying fatalism at work. To prevent the fulfillment of the prophecy, Laius had his newly born son's ankles pierced through and bound together so that he could not crawl; Jocasta then gave the boy to a servant to abandon, exposed to the elements on the nearby mountain range of Cithareon. However, the servant could not leave the child to die and gave the baby to a shepherd from Corinth, who then gave the infant to another shepherd until Oedipus eventually arrived at King Polybus and Queen Merope of Corinth. The king and queen of Corinth were childless and decided to adopt him and name him Oedipus after his swollen and injured feet.[35]

In a chance encounter with a drunkard at a banquet years later, Oedipus is told that he is illegitimate. He confronts his adopted parents, Polybus and Merope, with this revelation which they strongly deny. Oedipus, in that union between free will and fate, seeks out the same seer, the Oracle of Apollo at Delphi, that, unbeknownst to him, his biological parents Laius and Jocasta, had consulted. The oracle tells Oedipus that he is fated to murder his father and marry his mother. To avoid this miserable destiny, Oedipus *freely* seeks to outwit it, deciding not to return home to whom he believes are his biological parents in Corinth, but to travel to Thebes which was nearest where he was in Delphi, and unknowingly where his biological parents are, the very father he is fated to kill, and the mother he is fated to marry. At a crossroad, Oedipus, upset about the news from the Oracle, came near the town of Daulis, where three roads crossed each other. There he encountered a chariot, unbeknownst to him, conveying his biological father, King Laius. Oedipus is told by the king's men to step aside. Oedipus refuses out of anger and foolish pride. His refusal causes an altercation with Laius striking Oedipus, and Oedipus striking him back, killing him. There is only one witness to the murder, one of Laius' servants, who runs away. After the altercation and murder, Oedipus continues his journey to Thebes not realizing he has completed

---

[34] Aristotle, *Poetics*, 1460a26-30.

[35] "Oedipus" is rooted in the Greek word for swelling/oedema, where you would get the English word "edema."

the first half of the prophecy and thus, by killing his father, setting himself up to complete the second half of the prophecy, laying with his mother.

Oedipus encounters the Sphinx who was terrorizing the countryside around Thebes. The Sphinx would refuse travelers to pass unless they answered his riddle, destroying and eating those unable to answer it. If they were able to answer it, they were free to continue their journeys. The riddle: "what animal walks on four feet in the morning, two in the afternoon and three at night?" Oedipus is able to answer the riddle and thus *freely* continue toward his fate: "Man: as an infant, he crawls on all fours; as an adult, he walks on two legs and in old age, he uses a walking stick." Oedipus was the first to answer the riddle correctly which sets him up to be the new King of Thebes. Jocasta's brother, Creon (Oedipus' biological uncle unbeknownst to Oedipus) announced that any person who could outwit the Sphinx, and rid Thebes of its terror, would become the new king of Thebes and be given the just-widowed Queen Jocasta's hand in marriage. This marriage thus fulfilled the Oracle of Delphi's prophecy. Oedipus and Jocasta have four "cursed" children: two sons, Eteocles and Polynices (both central figures fighting each other for control of Thebes in Aeschylus' tragedy *Seven Against Thebes*), and two daughters, Antigone and Ismene (who factor prominently in the tragedy *Antigone*).

We see the totalizing entwining of fate and free will. Every single action committed by Oedipus is freely chosen. He is utterly responsible and, because he is responsible, he *can* be judged as he judges himself severely in the Theban cycle. This question of judgment is crucial to monotheism and to the possibility of a paradisal abode or, for that matter a place of torment such as Hell. Yet, the overarching strong theology of Apollo's fate upon them is irresistible all the same, calling to mind the strong theological power that we see in the Christian monotheistic vision of the universe. Oedipus freely consents to the actions and events before him, yet the presence of fate is guiding throughout, but guiding *without* violating freewill. The tension of free will and fate is startling: (1) Oedipus did not have to listen to the Oracle; (2) he could have returned to Corinth and the parents who raised him; (3) he did not have to kill the man (soon to be revealed as his father); (4) he did not have to marry Jocasta (soon to be revealed as his mother); (5) he could have listened to Tiresias and prodded no further; (6) he could have listened to his wife, Jocasta, and her pleas not to continue his investigation into his parents. We have a nascent structure which reflects the Christian understanding of a God Whose hand is ever-present, decisive, guiding, Whose judgment is all knowing, predestined, irresistible and inescapable, yet each human player has all the free will to expend and to be responsible for the outcome of divine judgment. The divine judgment is already decided, for God knows and judges all beyond time. Without this transcendent *beyond* time of the monotheistic Godhead, we do not have the metaphysical strength to ensure that Paradise is real, is distinct, is raised above earth and time. The structure in Oedipus is foreshadowing the Christian edifice of judgment, freedom, and afterlife.

A fatalistic worldview believes that all the essential forces which inform, create, shape, guide, punish and reward human life are out of human control. There is something else out there, it may the gods, the cosmogonic powers of existence, or a single Being, which sets game of life in play determining all events from the beginning until we are led to death. In fate, something non-human is in control of the game of life, the universe is not some random chance concatenation of events. The key here is that in fate, there is an overarching meaning or story to tell. In chance, while we cannot control things either, it differs from fate insofar as we cannot learn from it. This arbitrary mixing of situations and events is wholly estranged from a higher-order unifying meaning. But fate is not necessarily a pessimistic worldview. Tragedies often evoke fate where the divine force takes delight in human suffering and has little regard for the humans who are fated to certain outcomes. Sometimes fate is seen as a comfort, as lovers are "destined" to meet and fall in love. As if the forces of fate are benevolent and, if so, if I act justly and in harmony with the fate imposed around me, I can lead a contented life, perhaps even being rewarded with the source of true freedom and happiness in the afterlife. Whether the view of fate is pessimistic or benevolent, remember there is no human power to change the rules of the game of life. But a fatalistic worldview does not deny human freedom. The fates do control entirely the good and bad actions to happen and even to death – as Oedipus is fated to die in the sacred place of the Erinyes in *Oedipus at Colonus* – but this is the external framework of action. The internal or interior disposition, where freedom must originate, is not destroyed. The persons within a fatalistic worldview are not wholly deterministic. They can confront the experiences of their own fated plan; they can choose an attitude or disposition as to how to view it, as we see Job does in the Old Testament.

In fate we can still be held responsible. Persons bound by fate can attempt to make choices to avoid or outwit fate, can choose to accept, or reject it. In this sense, the gods can still hold those fated responsible. Did you play well, accept the rules of the game as well as you could? This bound-up-in-fate reality, where the freedom and responsibility of choosing well, playing the game of life well, is entirely written into the promise of Salvation in Christianity. We see this in *Ephesians* 1:

> Praise be to the God and Father of our Lord Jesus Christ, who has blessed us
> in the heavenly realms with every spiritual blessing in Christ. For he chose us
> in him before the creation of the world to be holy and blameless in his sight. In

love he predestined us for adoption to sonship through Jesus Christ, in accordance with his pleasure and will – to the praise of his glorious grace, which he has freely given us in the One he loves ... In him we were also chosen, having been predestined according to the plan of him who works out everything in conformity with the purpose of his will, in order that we, who were the first to put our hope in Christ, might be for the praise of his glory. And you also were included in Christ when you heard the message of truth, the gospel of your salvation. When you believed, you were marked in him with a seal, the promised Holy Spirit, who is a deposit guaranteeing our inheritance until the redemption of those who are God's possession – to the praise of his glory.[36]

It is not an unlimited freedom, but what freedom ever is? Aren't we still to this day "fated" to some extent by our family upbringing, our education, our genetics, our past, or motivations which may exist subconsciously? Both the great and the mediocre basketball player must play by the rules of the game. What differentiates them is not that one breaks the rules; their freedom has never been unlimited freedom without rules. What differentiates them is *how* they play or respond to the rules of the game. We consider them free while simultaneously enacting the rules, the "fate" structure of the game. When Sartre rejects God it is precisely because he sees the existence of any divine or governing being, no matter how benevolent, any providential order to existence as removing true human freedom, which needs a kind of virginal futurity. If God exists, then the plan is known and thus, in a way, fated in advance, there is a future but an increasingly unfree future. Sartre unites God with the notion of human nature or a human essence. For God to see, ordain, know and in a way be the cause of our futurity, because He creates our natures/essences, denies that we have a real future, a future not yet mapped out and if this be the case, our freedom is a mere play, a theatrical spectacle but not real. Thus, for Sartre, all freedom related to fate/God is like a castrated freedom. The free desire is there to take an attitude toward fate, but that freedom is always subsumed by the overriding inability to act or complete outside what was fated. The existence of God in conjunction with the natures God creates renders freedom impotent; human freedom cannot compete with any sense of the divine which, for Sartre, is likened to a kind of fate that maps out existence, and by doing so, undermines freedom. "The concept of man in the mind of God is comparable to the concept of a papercutter in the mind of the manufacturer ... thus the individualized man is the realization of a certain concept in the divine intelligence."[37]

Contra Sartre, how does one have freedom at all, or a freedom that *isn't* impotent without, as Plato knew it, some genuine directionality to existence, where one

---

[36] Eph. 1:3–14.   [37] Sartre, *Existentialism Is a Humanism*, 35.

choice is better than the next? And is not that directionality akin to fate? If there are no natures, no directions guiding existence, then every choice is as "good" as the next. In this situation, how am I free? Aren't we back within the problem of chance, where there is no overarching meaning to anything, everything in a way is arbitrary, in this instance there is no completion or fulfillment to my actions, which is phenomenologically the *experience* of freedom? Even when I ask questions such as "what should I do?" "how should I act to bring about the best end?" do not such questions (which imply freedom because they imply the human person as free agent) also simultaneously invoke an order or structure, indeed an overarching direction, or even fate? Aren't they invoking a better end, versus a worse one, to the given situation? Does not that directional action bind us, to make the choice is to bind us to it, is it not a kind of fate or at least companion to it? Isn't this precisely the point of Plato's *Myth of Er* in the *Republic*, when the dead pick their fates in the next life, more often foolishly than wisely? In *Oedipus Rex*, how Oedipus confronts his fate is the exercise of free will. For Sartre how I confront my radical freedom is my fate, "I am condemned to be free."[38]

The mystery of Christian predestination is pre-thematically reflected in Oedipus. As Oedipus exercises his freedom by the interior disposition confronting his fate, Christ has ordained through His body that same experience. Whether one is rich or poor, lives a lengthy or brief life, it is the disposition of the soul to the inescapability of Christ as singular final judge: "I am the resurrection and the life. The one who believes in me will live, even though they die; and whoever lives by believing in me will never die. Do you believe this?"[39] We see this strong metaphysical reality supported by the Angelic Doctor:

> It seems that men are not predestined by God, for Damascene says (De Fide Orth. ii, 30): "It must be borne in mind that God foreknows but does not predetermine everything, since He foreknows all that is in us, but does not predetermine it all." But human merit and demerit are in us, forasmuch as we are the masters of our own acts by free will. All that pertains therefore to merit or demerit is not predestined by God; and thus man's predestination is done away.[40]

St. Thomas' response to the objector is to argue that because human beings are capable of eternal life via gift/grace, and not by our own powers, predestination helps move us toward the end of life that is supernatural. Thus, predestination is not merely foreknowledge but fore-movement, fore-inclining the rational creature toward its end.[41] Predestination is a plan, existing in God's mind, an

---

[38] Sartre, *Being and Nothingness*, 663.   [39] Jn. 11:25–26.   [40] ST I, 23, 1, Obj. 1.

[41] Cf. ST I, 23, 1, ad. 1: "I answer that, it is fitting that God should predestine men. For all things are subject to His providence, as was shown above (I:22:2). Now it belongs to providence to direct things towards their end, as was also said (I:22:1 and I:22:2). The end towards which created things are directed by God is twofold; one which exceeds all proportion and faculty of created

ordering of persons to salvation. The exercise of this plan is passively carried out in the persons predestined, though actively in God. Because God is metaphysical Being or Existence itself, in the unity of Being there is no distinction between what flows from free will, and what is from predestination. God's causation produces effects which, when we participate in them, are actively experienced as our free will, and also passively ordered via God's predestination of us, as well as experienced by us – often in hindsight – in our recognition of providential acts. And, again, because God is Being/Existence itself (thus there is only God's plan) nothing can thwart His Divine Will.

From *Oedipus Rex* to its heights in Christian monotheism, here is the uneasy, yet essential, paradox: (A) humans have free will and (B) God's sovereignty as Being Itself is that the Divine Plan cannot be thwarted by our human volition. But, for St. Thomas, God's existential/sovereign will does not negate or lessen our freedom in the way that Sartre would describe God, as the puppeteer of a Punch and Judy play, pulling the strings behind all our choices. Human beings are always in varying degrees of recognition in the presence of God's sovereign Will, we are free to accept it or reject it without God's will forcing us into either choice. This is our free response to God. But our freedom to choose is also within the existential omniscience of God. Since God is omniscient, He has always prearranged his Sovereign Will according to His soteriological (ultimate) purpose for each of us, so that our freedom born from within the existence of His Will does not undermine His ultimate purpose. And his ultimate purpose is our freedom as happiness as Paradisal promise.

In the *Oedipus* cycle, the collision of fate and free will hinges on the choices that lead to death – from the murder of Laius to Jocasta's suicide to Oedipus' own sacrifice in *Oedipus at Colonus*, and Antigone's in *Antigone*. Death is the decisive reminder of fate as present reality, and central to a monotheistic view where God can overcome its irrevocability. We may live longer than those in medieval times, have vaccines and medicines to lengthen the game of fate, but death itself is the fatal omnipresent force throughout our lives which we cannot master. The denial of fate was a product of the very recent, historically speaking,

---

nature; and this end is life eternal, that consists in seeing God which is above the nature of every creature, as shown above (1:12:4). The other end, however, is proportionate to created nature, to which end created being can attain according to the power of its nature. Now if a thing cannot attain to something by the power of its nature, it must be directed thereto by another; thus, an arrow is directed by the archer towards a mark. Hence, properly speaking, a rational creature, capable of eternal life, is led towards it, directed, as it were, by God. The reason of that direction pre-exists in God; as in Him is the type of the order of all things towards an end, which we proved above to be providence. Now the type in the mind of the doer of something to be done, is a kind of pre-existence in him of the thing to be done. Hence the type of the aforesaid direction of a rational creature towards the end of life eternal is called predestination. For to destine, is to direct or send. Thus it is clear that predestination, as regards its objects, is a part of providence."

Enlightenment Project of the seventeenth and eighteenth centuries. Western civilization now has a great aversion to viewing the world as evoking a fatalistic worldview, whether that's through divine powers or other powers outside of our control. Still, the world, again and again, reminds us that there are binding and controlling forces more powerful, mysterious, and misunderstood than we can imagine. These forces, from pandemics to natural disasters, to tragic deaths which if only the person had left 5 minutes earlier, remind us that very little is under human control. Perhaps, it is quite true that to be human, we also needed the Promethean gift of delusion that allowed us to live and act without the constant focus on the fatal power of death. *Oedipus Rex* is precisely making this point, that human knowledge and power are always limited, so either the rest of life's control is governed by fate or chance, for Sophocles, since chance disallows making sense of anything in its randomness, then fate better reflects how humans seek to find meaning in all situations.

Many years after Oedipus married Jocasta, a terrible plague of infertility befell the city of Thebes, affecting all things in its wake, from crops, livestock, to people. Oedipus asserted that *he* would figure out a strategy to stop the pestilence entirely. He has stopped the Sphinx, he is the leader, the *tyrannos*, who can get the job done. He sends Creon (his brother in-law, but actual biological uncle) to the same Oracle of Apollo at Delphi, seeking advice. Creon returns informing Oedipus that justice must be paid; that the murderer of the former King Laius must be brought to justice. The hero appears to be the one who confronts fate in a very intimate, personal, and profound manner with dramatic consequences, and whose reaction to that encounter with fate serves to cast light on the human condition. Oedipus is a beloved leader at a moment of crisis. Thebes has been attacked by a mysterious plague, something which is a manifestation of the fatal forces of existence. The people and their livelihoods are dying; they need to stop the disaster. They turn to Oedipus, their firm and popular ruler. Oedipus is respected for his wisdom, is given great political power, as the priest clearly relays to Oedipus in the following lines:

> We consider you foremost among men
> in the hazards of life, and when we have to deal
> with powers more than human.[42]

This passage foreshadows why Apollo has fated Oedipus to be made a supreme example to the people of Thebes, who have undermined the gods by their *hubris*. Oedipus is a person of endless self-assurance and self-confidence bordering on *hubris*, but in the game of fate it is this boundless self-assurance which makes him

---

[42] Sophocles, *Oedipus Rex*, 37–39.

a beloved leader. He describes himself as "renowned in the eyes of all," and thus can take on *full* responsibility for dealing with the crisis, a task and challenge he relishes. Oedipus curses the killer of his wife Jocasta's late husband, arguing that such a person would be exiled. The meaning of exile here is deeply symbolic, akin to such alienation as to be buried outside of holy land – which is exactly what Oedipus will inflict upon himself in *Oedipus at Colonus*. Oedipus freely sends himself to his own fated end, not unlike a martyrological act in Christianity. Creon then advises Oedipus to seek out the revered blind prophet for additional guidance. Oedipus sends for him, but Tiresias repeatedly warns him not to seek out and discover Laius' killer. In an angered exchange, Oedipus provokes Tiresias into revealing the truth, that Oedipus is the curse, Oedipus was the killer, and then Tiresias proceeds to taunt Oedipus saying that the king does not even know who his biological parents are. Tiresias answers in riddles only, stating that King Laius' murderer will be both brother and father to his children, both son and husband to his mother. Oedipus does not yet connect the dots, becomes deeply angry and confronts Creon for bringing Tiresias to him with, what he *still* considers, slanderous false accusations. Oedipus accuses Creon of trying to overthrow him and take the throne, which was not what was *happening at all*, but does *actually* happen at the end of the play when Creon becomes King. Again, Oedipus freely sends himself to his own fated end, not unlike a martyrological act in Christianity.

This fusing of fate and free will culminating in a martyrological destiny is the historical pattern of Christianity. It is the movement of surrender in hopes of a Paradisal reality which *can* offer justice, and balance what cannot be satisfied on earth. Nothing on earth can fulfill the demands of our freedom and our fate. We see this reality beginning to materialize in *Oedipus Rex*. The prophet Tiresias' *very being* foreshadows the odd position of human person *in* but not *of* the word. Tiresus' being gives us a foretaste of the fate that Oedipus will inflict upon himself culminating in *Oedipus at Colonus* – blinded and exiled, a prophetic figure neither here nor there. In varying ancient accounts Tiresias. through punishment from the gods, is exiled from his own sex, becomes a woman, and then is returned to a man. He is blinded but given the gift of foresight in compensation. Tiresias is also fated by his own fore-knowledge and inability to change the course of life. His very presence foreshadows what Oedipus will become.

> And since you mock my blindness, I say
> you see all right but not the evil you're in
> or where you live, or whom you live with. Do you know
> your origins? You don't even know that you
> are loathsome to your kin, both those beneath

and those upon the earth. Your mother's and father's
double curse will hound you from this land
one day, in terror – sighted now, but seeing
darkness then. What refuge for your cries?[43]

Christianity's Paradisal promise functions on the backdrop of an ironic fate and free will – the first shall be the last, the last shall be the first, sight is blindness, blindness is sight:

> Jesus said, "For judgment I have come into this world, so that the blind will see and those who see will become blind." Some Pharisees who were with him heard him say this and asked, "What? Are we blind too?" Jesus said, "If you were blind, you would not be guilty of sin; but now that you claim you can see, your guilt remains."[44]

In *Oedipus Rex*, Oedipus has spent his entire life with the issue of ironic fate and free will pressing at him. We know he was told before he went to Thebes that he is fated to kill his father and marry his mother. And he freely refused to accept that fate. He freely moved away to avoid his fate which he found morally reprehensible. The audience can support Oedipus' pull of free will to avoid his fate. We also see that this so-called avoidance of fate has rendered him overly self-confident so that Oedipus becomes the perfect symbol of *hubris* and the consequences thereof which result when thinking one can freely outwit the gods as designated by the gods before his birth. Oedipus believes he has acquired the knowledge to master the fates. This is the *hubris* underneath all civilizational downfalls, upon which all dystopias, are built – that the human person does not have to obey limited freedom and submit to an unwelcome fate. Because Oedipus believes he has changed his life's direction, it gives him all those powerful reasons for being so self-assured in his abilities to deal with the unknown mysteries and powers which control the world.

Oedipus is blind when he sees, and only sees when he is blinded. This is the irony of the play. Oedipus is deceived on how human and divine relationships work, on how free will and fate intermingle. This image of blindness is utilized to define philosophy in the *Republic* as the ascent of the soul from the day that is night to the night which is actually true day. In a word, what is falsehood to those who cannot see is actually daylight/truth. And what is daylight/truth to those who cannot see is actually night/untruth.[45] Oedipus who thinks he can see has

---

[43] Sophocles, *Oedipus Rex*, 412–20.   [44] Jn. 9:39–41.
[45] In Plato's "Allegory of the Cave," *Republic* VII, Plato gives us an elaborate image of this definition: "And if there were a contest, and he had to compete in measuring the shadows with the prisoners who had never moved out of the den, while his sight was still weak, and before his eyes had become steady (and the time which would be needed to acquire this new habit of sight might be very considerable) would he not be ridiculous? Men would say of him that up he went and

been blind the whole time calling to mind the passage above in John. Oedipus now knows who he is, who his parents are, and that he has fulfilled the prophecy. He screams in the presence of this truth and flees inside the palace.

> Oedipus: Why, then, did you give him to this old man?
> Shepherd: Out of pity, master. I thought he'd take him
> away, where he is from. But he
> has saved him for the worst of fates. For if
> you're who he says you are, you were born doomed.
> Oedipus: *iou, iou!* It's all come out too clear. Light,
> may I never look upon you again! I'm the one
> born to those I shouldn't have come from, living with those
> I shouldn't live with, killing those I ought not have killed.[46]

Ironically, Oedipus is the rightful heir to the throne, but he loses it, in a way, for not being the rightful heir due to killing his father, being his mother's husband, being his children's brother, thus perverting the orders which enable rightful heirs. In the Christian vision of Salvation, we are the heirs – God desires to save all, each is the inheritor of the Kingdom – but we can freely lose our inheritance by *how* we respond to the great design, by loving our lives more when they are but shadows of life, losing sight that death is life, what is down is up, that we may be blind when we see. This radical inverted structure is cultivated in *Oedipus Rex* where sight is blindness, and blindness to sight under the design of fate bonded to free will. These paradoxical layers are then raised up within Christianity, ultimately preparing us to accept the ultimate reversal: beyond blindness as sight, death is what brings Paradise and eternal life.

> Jesus strictly warned them not to tell this to anyone. And he said, "The Son of Man must suffer many things and be rejected by the elders, the chief priests and the teachers of the law, and he must be killed and on the third day be raised to life." Then he said to them all: "Whoever wants to be my disciple must deny themselves and take up their cross daily and follow me. For whoever wants to save their life will lose it, but whoever loses their life for me will save it. What good is it for someone to gain the whole world, and yet lose or forfeit their very self? Whoever is ashamed of me and my words, the Son of Man will be ashamed of them when he comes in his glory and in the glory of the Father and of the holy angels. Truly I tell you, some who are standing here will not taste death before they see the kingdom of God."[47]

---

down he came without his eyes; and that it was better not even to think of ascending; and if any one tried to loose another and lead him up to the light, let them only catch the offender, and they would put him to death."

[46] Sophocles, *Oedipus Rex*, 1177–85.   [47] Lk. 9:21–27.

Whereas Christian monotheism in its apex in Christ fulfills the relationship between fate and free will overcoming a pessimistic view of fate, we do not have that same perfection for Oedipus. In essence, this inescapable entwining of fate and free will, which marks human life, cannot be emancipated fully from a negative view without the strong theology of Revelation which offers Salvation. Only Paradise can unite the overarching necessity of fate with the conditional reality of free will, giving each absolute dignity in a structure where the latter does not lose out to the former, but gains its freedom as completion. Oedipus on the other hand uses his free will to find the truth, fate, but truth cannot set him free as it does in the Christian promise of Salvation. There is no revealed monotheistic Godhead Who *Is*, and Who is Truth itself, freeing the person for Truth as His body, as we experience in Christ. Instead, Oedipus persists in believing he cannot be the one who has brought about this pestilence, even though he recalls killing a man at a three-way crossroads. Thus, he persists in finding the truth even as Jocasta begs him to stop. Truth becomes obsessional: in the end, the truth itself is more important than what that truth might reveal and what costs it might incur. This is not a benevolent but an extremely pessimistic view of fate. Oedipus is, for the most part, an exemplary and great man; he doesn't possess duplicity and is filled with good intentions to save his city. In a way fundamental and profound, Oedipus is mostly innocent. His fate was sealed by the gods *before* his birth. He has done nothing knowingly to be punished with such a fate, except that he does freely commit the sins that flesh out the architecture of fate, namely killing his father and acting with *hubris*. All the course of events which lead him to learn the truth about his origins have been freely initiated by his own free choices. This vision of life is merciless and unfathomable. This is a good man, existentially innocent, subjected to such a terrible fate. This is a pessimistic fatalism because there is no covenant between man and God (perhaps not until *Oedipus at Colonus*), no sense that Oedipus' fate is linked to atone his own personal sins, or that there is some sense of reward, a promise of happiness in the future, as one would see of the various Covenants in the Bible.

This pessimistic view, where truth materializing in the revelation of fate and free will, is seen clearly in and after Jocasta's death. Jocasta, unable to live, hangs herself and Oedipus blinds himself. She has locked herself in her room, weeping for her dead husband Laius and lamenting the horrendous fate ensnaring their family. Oedipus bangs on the door in a rage, demanding a sword and, cursing Jocasta, he hurls his weight at the door and bursts through where his eyes fall upon Jocasta hanging lifeless from a noose. Oedipus weeps and cradles Jocasta's body, then takes the golden pins that held her robes together and proceeds to stab his eyes until there is nothing left. He plunges the pins in and runs them up and down his eyes, crying out how he is unable to bear any sight of the world after having learned that he has not escaped the prophecy but completed it in all its evil. In *Oedipus Rex*, there is no covenant, no Paradise where fate completes human freedom, instead fate has competed with human freedom and won:

> And there, we saw the woman hanging, swinging
> in the air, entangled in a twisted noose.
> And when he saw her, in his grief he cried out
> a dreadful groan, then loosed the hanging halter.
> And when the poor woman lay upon the ground,
> it was dreadful to see, what happened next. He tore from her
> the golden brooches that pinned her clothes, raised them up
> and dashed them against his eyes, crying out
> that from now on those eyes would not see him
> or the evils he had done and suffered, but see
> in darkness those whom he should not have seen,
> and not know those he had wanted to know.[48]

Oedipus blinds himself to reclaim an act of free will outside what has been fated for him. With blood streaming from his injured and blinded eyes, Oedipus angrily laments this fate as well as the eternal night that now surrounds him. Remember, Oedipus' fate was determined by the gods prior to his birth, he was to symbolize those who, through *hubris*, undermine the influence of the gods and of their religious obligations. Oedipus exclaims that it may have been Apollo, the god of plagues, who directed his destiny, but he *alone* blinded his own eyes. Here freedom is present, but it cannot issue in perfection, it can only respond to the pessimism and the loss. Oedipus desires to be forever exiled from Thebes; the Chorus shrinks in witnessing him curse his life in its entirety – birth, marriage, and all the members related to him. Again, Oedipus may be enacting his freedom against fate, but the tension between these two poles will only terminate in pessimism. In *Oedipus Rex*, we have the opposite of the God who can redeem, we do not have the Christian singular godhead liberating the person into perfection. Instead, we have freedom embodied in blind Oedipus raging against Apollonian fate:

> This was Apollo, my friends; Apollo
> brought these evils to pass, my evils,
> these my sufferings.
> But no hand struck my eyes, none
> but mine, mine alone!
> For why should I go on seeing, I
> who had, when seeing, nothing sweet to see?[49]

---

[48] Sophocles, *Oedipus Rex*, 1263–74.   [49] Sophocles, *Oedipus Rex*, 1329–36.

2.3 Oedipus and Tragic Meaning

What then is the Tragic in relation to Fate? Is Oedipus a tragic figure *because* of his defiance in the face of fate, his free will attitude of refusal to accept his fate? He does not align himself to his fate as Moses or Job or St. John the Baptist, or most profoundly Christ does. Oedipus answers only to himself, we see this in his attitude toward the Oracle, Tiresias, and Jocasta. Oedipus will shape his life by his own rules, no one else's, not even mysterious powers he cannot as yet understand. Instead, he will find a way to understand them and make them submit to him, as in the case of the Sphinx and the plague. At no point in the play is he willing to compromise. Oedipus is to be admired because this refusal to play by anyone else's rules does evoke a noble morality: he never conceals what he is feeling, he isn't duplicitous like Creon. What you see is what *is*. Oedipus' greatness manifests itself throughout his very being and in everything he does. Still, this defiance in the face of fate and his belief that he has outwitted his abhorrent fate have fed his enormous almost tyrannical self-confidence which closes off dissenting views and advice, but at the same time he is *always* nobly prepared to accept all the consequences for his actions. The Chorus blames the gods, blames fate, blames everyone else *but* Oedipus. But being largely free from blame does not gift Oedipus with a union of fate and free will that is positive as in Christian Salvation. Oedipus reminds us of the steps needed to arrive at a positive view of the union of those two poles. Like Oedipus, martyrological Christianity sees agapeic surrender coming from free choice as master of our reactions, even as, with Oedipus, fate swallows us up and completes its mission as it does repeatedly in death. The paradoxical structure of Christianity is revealed: Paradise comes through death, comes through the eternal life awarded through death, it is the choosing to take total responsibility as fate engulfs and seemingly overwhelms responsibility. Oedipus blinds himself, then he asks to be exiled, and for his daughters to be spared, he therefore chooses free will, to remain the master of what happens to him. The responsibility is his own. He refuses to let fate remove his role, his greatness, in all the events that unfolded.

The tragedy of the play is not Oedipus' sufferings per se, many a non-tragic figure has suffered in the course of history. The tragedy arises from the connection between Oedipus' sufferings in relation to his own freely chosen actions throughout the play, combined with the audience's awareness that Oedipus is bringing himself closer to the inevitable, dreadful fated outcome. His freely chosen decisions are – unbeknownst to him but known to us – bringing events closer to that inevitable horrendous conclusion. But Oedipus is free to go in different directions; he is not compelled to do what he does. As we look over the play we see, strangely enough, these inevitable consequences arising from Oedipus' free decisions.

Some key points in the relationship between Tragedy and the hope for Paradise in Christian monotheism:

1. Chance is not Tragic *per se*: In a literary sense, a truly chance accident may be horrible, pathetic, heartrending, but is never "tragic." They are accidents of blind, indifferent cosmogonic chance. What embodies *Oedipus Rex* is the collision between fate and free will, the clear link between Oedipus, the hero's own free choices throughout the play and the disastrous fate that completes those free choices. *Oedipus Rex* is a supreme example of tragedy because of this intermingling of free will and sheer inevitability. In a weak theology where God cannot intervene, we may have chance, unexpected events, but we do not have the tragic sense of life that can issue existentially in the desire for Heaven and the power of paradise to shape this earthly life.

2. Oedipus is fated primarily because he is the sort of person to be doomed. There is an intrinsic goodness that evokes the Christian demands for martyrological hope and Sainthood. Another person, Creon for example, someone with a very different character, would not have suffered Oedipus' fate. Many would have compromised their sense of freedom in the name of a multitude of different things, from prudence, to saving face, to political survival. The strong monotheism of Christianity and its promise of Salvation evoke a need for aspects of the Christ-like in its representatives. Because of the agonic paradoxical structure at root in Christianity, the desire for Paradise is achieved through heroic act and vision. If free will is able to survive the power of fate, and life is to come from death, if these things are to be endured and believed and sought after, then it takes a figure such as Oedipus to bring these poles into dialogic unmissable reality.

3. Vanity of Vanities: Is the hidden moral of the tragedy that any person who sets him/herself up as wholly free, as master of his/her fate will, cannot outwit the demands of existence and will come to a self-destructive end? Fate is always more powerful and complex than any human mind in its limited understanding can acknowledge or master. The world may delude us into thinking we have become masters of fate, but this is the vanity of vanities. The strong theology of Christian monotheism does not compete in a pessimistic manner with free will, but the pessimistic view still encroaches and threatens to overwhelm. This is why we can name persons in Heaven, for example, but the Church has never listed one person we know in Hell. "Thy Will be done" is fate transformed into Person. Christ becomes "thy will be done" enduring that fate to

His death. His sacrifice unites fate and free will in a positive view, but it takes His death and resurrection to transform the overriding pessimistic end of *Oedipus Rex*'s maintenance of freedom. "Father, if you are willing, take this cup from me; yet not my will, but yours be done"[50] necessitated the sacrifice beyond all sacrifices that Oedipus senses in Colonus, but only fate as Person could complete in absolute freedom, and only then could the hope for Paradise enter into the historical appetite of mankind.

Blind Oedipus desires that the cup of suffering not fall on his daughters, that it pass, that his own being take on all the sins of the family, that it ends with him, begs for Creon's paternal protection over his family. But we know this will not be fulfilled, Oedipus does not have the power to marry fate and freedom completely, his body cannot become Paradise as Christ's Is.[51] Oedipus states that his sons, Eteocles and Polynices, are grown up and able to fend for themselves, but he requests that Creon watch over his daughters, Antigone and Ismene, whom he asks to "see" one last time before he embarks on his exile.

> And I weep – I can't see but I weep
> for you – the bitterness of the days ahead,
> how people will treat you from now on.[52]

Antigone and Ismene come to Oedipus weeping, he embraces them also weeping, in deep sadness that his malediction curses them – that society will exclude them, men will not marry them. Oedipus asks his daughters to pray for a better life than his own. Oedipus, again, asks Creon to watch over his daughters. He reaches to touch Creon, but Creon refuses Oedipus' hand. Creon, the new king/tyrant, puts a stop the goodbyes, saying that Oedipus' weeping has become shameful. Creon orders his men to remove Antigone and Ismene away from Oedipus as Oedipus begs for them to stay. Creon tells Oedipus that his power has ended and to cease desiring it. The Chorus having the final word relays to us that the greatest of men has fallen, that life is fraught with misery and only the grave can bring peace.

---

[50] Lk 22:42.

[51] Cf. ST III, 10, 2, *resp*: "It must be said that the soul of Christ knows all things in the Word. For every created intellect knows in the Word, not all simply, but so many more things the more perfectly it sees the Word. Yet no beatified intellect fails to know in the Word whatever pertains to itself. Now to Christ and to His dignity all things to some extent belong, inasmuch as all things are subject to Him. Moreover, He has been appointed Judge of all by God, 'because He is the Son of Man,' as is said John 5:27; and therefore the soul of Christ knows in the Word all things existing in whatever time, and the thoughts of men, of which He is the Judge, so that what is said of Him (John 2:25), 'For He knew what was in man,' can be understood not merely of the Divine knowledge, but also of His soul's knowledge, which it had in the Word."

[52] Sophocles, *Oedipus Rex*, 1485–87.

Don't let their sorrows be as great as mine.
Take pity on them, seeing them, so young,
bereft of all, unless you take their part.
Show that you agree with a touch of your hand![53]

In *Oedipus at Colonus*, Oedipus is a prophetic presence, understanding the fates that will befall members of his family, and the city of Thebes. He is wandering blind, guided by Antigone into a village deemed sacred by the *Erinyes*, the deities of vengeance. They demand he leaves, but Oedipus knows he must stay. The other part of the Delphi's prophecy to him was that he will die in such a land and be a blessing for the land where he is buried. The true loathsome character of Creon is revealed, Oedipus' sons, Eteocles and Polynices, walk into their fate, and Athens in his death is blessed. In *Antigone,* Oedipus' two grown sons, Eteocles and Polynices, each take opposing sides in the Theban civil war. The brothers kill each other, and Creon decides that Polynices was a traitor and should not be given burial rites, instead will be left unburied, shamed, and pickings for birds of prey. Refusing to accept this rule, Antigone attempted to bury her brother. In Sophocles' *Antigone*, Creon had her buried in a rock cavern for defying him, whereupon she hanged herself. There is freedom in the Theban plays but, in the heavy hands of fate, it cannot be enacted in any other way but a pessimistic view. It takes the radically strong yoking of paradoxes as seen only in the God-Man – fully God and fully man, undying and dying, eternity and time, fate and freedom, father and son – to produce the joy and abundance needed for the hope for Salvation and the metaphysical foundation of Paradise.

At the moment of the Agony and of the Passion He can no longer enter there [his nest of refuge in the Father], He is barred from it by uncrossable barriers, this is why He feels himself abandoned. That has been the supreme exemplar of the night of the spirit of the mystics, the absolutely complete night. The whole world of the Vision and of the divinized supraconscious was there, but He no longer experienced it at all through His infused contemplation. And likewise, the radiance and the influx of this world on the entire soul were more powerful than ever, but were no longer seized at all by the consciousness, nor experienced. Jesus was more than ever united with the Father, but in the terror and the sweat of blood, and in the experience of dereliction.[54]

3 Plato: The Difficulty of Paradise

"He will gladly take part in and enjoy those which he thinks will make him a better man, but in public and private life he will shun those that may overthrow the

---

[53] Sophocles, *Oedipus Rex*, 1507–10.
[54] Maritain, *The Grace and Humanity of Jesus Christ*, 61.

Figure 2 Gods and Fates.JPG, by Carol Scott

established habit of his soul." "Then, if that is his chief concern," he said, "he will not willingly take part in politics." "Yes, by the dog," said I, "in his own city he certainly will, yet perhaps not in the city of his birth, except in some providential conjuncture." "I understand," he said; "you mean the city whose establishment we have described, the city whose home is in the ideal; for I think that it can be found nowhere on earth." "Well," said I, "perhaps there is a pattern of it laid up in heaven for him who wishes to contemplate it and so beholding to constitute himself its citizen. But it makes no difference whether it exists now or ever will come into being. The politics of this city only will be his and of none other." "That seems probable," he said.

– Plato, Republic[55]

The discussions in Section 3 will continue the theme of justice now situated within the problem of the human soul. In terms of Plato, our inquiries into the nature of the soul, immortality, and the afterlife will emphasize why his understanding of the *polis* is essential to these matters. To do so, we must closely contrast the common understanding of the Platonic prison-house of the body in relation to the soul, with the development of the *polis* in all its failed forms in the

---

[55] Plato, *Republic*, 592a–b.

Republic and *Laws*. Emphasis on *eros*, *mythos*, *lysis*, will renew the analysis of the tragic in Section 2 but from a more fully realized anthropological position, one which renders the possibility of happiness as beyond all earthly powers.

3.1 Plato and the Body Politique of the Soul

> Greek philosophy purifies the soul and prepares it to receive the faith on which truth constructs knowledge.
>
> – St. Clement of Alexandria, *The Stromata*[56]

While there is no disputing that the metaphysical anthropology of Plato's understanding of the body and soul is one of irreconcilable division, when we confront his political order we see a different situatedness of body to spirit, and an analogy of the human person to society that is much more integrated. The metaphysical estrangement of body and soul combined with the political unifying of those polarities calls to mind a pre-Christian struggle with the end of the human person, and of the type of perfection befitting human nature. In essence, Plato is circling latently around questions of Paradise in monotheism.

The fundamental question of the *Republic* is how the formation of the *polis* (the city-state) relates to the human person and why this formation is radically essential to all understandings of life and death. There is not one facet of the *Republic* that is outside a theologically oriented interrogation of human nature. In the prologue, Plato discusses the state of the older and middle generations in relation to knowledge of the Good, leading us to the key existential status of the younger generation as represented by Glaucon and Adeimantus. The older generation, embodied by Cephalus, possessed the meaning of the Transcendentals as foundation for the soul and the soul of society but with a mixture of *mimesis*. The middle generation, embodied by Polemarchus, have been handed the Good only by *mimesis* (imitation) which leaves them unable to pass it down effectively to the younger generation. From the outset, the subtextual issue of *lysis*, how things fall apart, losing the efficacy of the good, is preoccupying the mind of the dialogue. This is crucial, because through it we can understand the interpretative apparatus where Plato is justly looking for a strong monotheism, a source which can withstand *lysis*, recover what is lost, a source that is Paradisal, as we see so centrally emphasized in Christianity. The younger generation, Glaucon and Adeimantus, are in a perilous position. Whereas the middle generation is floundering having only received the Good by *mimesis*, this generation, has the scraps of *mimesis*, an even more impotent rendering which cannot encourage the human person to conform, to desire to conform to the True, the Good, and the Beautiful.

---

[56] St. Clement of Alexandria, *The Stromata*, vii, 20.

The Good order can no longer be found in surrounding society and the younger generation have no model or guide for wisdom.

The question of handing down tradition raises what or who can maintain the movement of that tradition through time and change. The setting of the *Republic* is the generational reduction of the wisdom of justice: (1) old Cephalus is moved to discuss justice because of his nearing death and descent into Hades; (2) Polemarchus, has justice only by *mimesis*, according to others; (3) Glaucon and Adeimantus find no meaning in the empty *mimesis*. The younger generation is drawn to the tyrannical sophist Thrasymachus and his revolt because at least the search for meaning appears real and possesses an eroticism of promised roots, foundations, and truths. The younger generation seek the strong *radices*, the radical, the "root" that will orient their lives and turn away from *mimesis* because they instinctively recognize that it is a wilting flower, having been cut off from any root long ago.

The dialogue begins with a descent into the Athenian port town of Piraeus. This descent is a search for the theological ground which unites persons as one, as much as it is a turning away from an insufficient or false foundation. Socrates does not find the one God which can unite human polarities and can complete what sacrifice desires. The whole spectacle of the celebrations for the foreigners' Thracian goddess is placed on equal footing with the citizens Greek gods being praised. Socrates marvels at this, offers his prayers to the gods. Whereas in Athens, the Athenians and the Thracians were at odds, here they found their commonality – but it is a temporary commonality, one during the bacchanal not for daily life. This descent outlines the false equality of civilization unified by the lowest common denominator. If we place perfection on a worldly idea, money, status, family position, power, desires achieved, we will blind the soul to its true nature. Plato sees any form of false equality as a form of Death mirroring the imagery in the epilogue of the descent into Hades. The symbolism of descent to find union remains within the rest of the dialogue and its questions regarding true equality, the true unitive force that unites souls toward the good shared by each. The descent in the prologue will mirror the descent into Hades in the epilogue. We learn that equality cannot occur if it involves the death of the soul, the soul must live eternally, and it must be larger and more than it ever was. Again, what could possibly ensure the survival from decay, loss, death?

As stated, the descent into Piraeus in the prologue mirrors the Epilogue's Myth of Er, the Spindle of Necessity, where dead souls receive reward or punishment depending on their conduct in life. The souls are judged impartially, naked, so no earthly rank can sway the judge. Pamphylus, a war hero who has recently died watches the whole spectacle. Having not drunk from the river *lethe* (forgetfulness) he is allowed to come back to earth and tell what he has seen in the underworld. He sees the dead souls after centuries of either punishment or bliss assembled and choosing their fate for the next life. Souls will lead the lives they have chosen for themselves – again we see the theme of fate and free will entwined in the Spindle of Necessity.

> No divinity shall cast lots for you, but you shall choose your own deity. Let him to whom falls the first lot first select a life to which he shall cleave of necessity. But virtue has no master over her, and each shall have more or less of her as he honors her or does her despite. The blame is his who chooses: God is blameless. So saying, the prophet flung the lots out among them all, and each took up the lot that fell by his side, except himself; him they did not permit. And whoever took up a lot saw plainly what number he had drawn.[57]

The *arete* of the soul has no master and thus man has no one to blame but himself if he is punished. Pamphylus relays the following:

1. Those who suffered much tend to choose cautiously their next life;
2. Those who participated in Arete by habit (*mimesis*) only and thus were fortunate not suffer in the afterlife chose foolishly the nature of their next life;
3. The quality of life must be judged by its suitability to develop *arete* (virtue). Freedom is not much use unless it is honoring the Arete which invokes right decision.

In Piraeus, Socrates marvels at the equality among the Thracian foreigners and the Athenian citizens. But this equality at the harbor (where men forfeit their identities) would be the death of Athens which must build its culture (*paideia*) as an expression of the soul. In Hades, Pamphylus sees that all men are "everyman" all equal before their judge; one's power in this life has no sway in the next. The question remains: Must men remain in these underworlds, or do they have the power to ascend from death to life? If they do not, who can render this impossible but civilizational desire possible? There can be no false unity, no substitute for life over death. Plato is searching for that power to ground civilization, to form souls that we see in Isaiah:

> He will swallow up death for all time,
> And the Lord God will wipe tears away from all faces,
> And He will remove the reproach of His people from all the earth;
> For the Lord has spoken.[58]

This is the one of the central hopes of Christian monotheism, where all persons find unity and equality in Paradise through victory over death: "In him we have

---

[57] Plato, *Republic*, 618a.   [58] Is. 25:8.

redemption through his blood, the forgiveness of sins, in accordance with the riches of God's grace that he lavished on us."[59] But equality is often won through a freedom without substance, it is an "underworld" equality and not one where the human person can rise to know the Good in its fullness. In the *Republic*, much like in *Oedipus Rex*, we need a salvific figure who can endure these poles of tension, and bring one from death into life, merging the powers of fate and free will:

> The worthy disciples of philosophy will be but a small remnant, a small few ... Those who belong to this small class have tasted how sweet and blessed a possession philosophy is, and have also seen enough of the madness of the multitude; and they know that no politician is honest, nor is there any champion of justice at whose side they may fight and be saved. Such an one may be compared to a man who has fallen among wild beasts – he will not join in the wickedness of his fellows, but neither is he able singly to resist all their fierce natures, and therefore seeing that he would be of no use to the State or to his friends, and reflecting that he would have to throw away his life without doing any good either to himself or others, he holds his peace, and goes his own way. He is like one who, in the storm of dust and sleet which the driving wind hurries along, retires under the shelter of a wall; and seeing the rest of mankind full of wickedness, he is content, if only he can live his own life and be pure from evil or unrighteousness, and depart in peace and good-will, with bright hopes.[60]

For Plato, this is achieved through learning justice (*dike*); becoming friends to ourselves and to the gods, it is a purgation of ignorance through struggle. It is another manifestation and intensification of the Hymn to Zeus in the *Agamemnon*, of the suffering that brings enlightenment: "Zeus, who guided men to think, who has laid it down that wisdom comes alone through suffering."[61] Socrates is now the salvific helper, helping one ascend from death to life, from false wisdom to true wisdom (*phroenesis*) discovered in justice (*dike*). When we think of the Salvific helper, we are reminded of remarks by GK Chesterton: "The true soldier fights not because he hates what is in front of him, but because he loves what is behind him."[62] This motivating love of wisdom and foundation categorically differentiates Socrates from any tyranny or false leadership and rule. Contrasting the level ground of Piraeus, hierarchy and ascent become the erotic movement of the dialogue. The first step of ascent from death (either Piraeus or Hades) is to find the salvific helper. Socrates is the metaphysician and the physician. He helps diagnose the right and wrong paradigms of life. The Socratic physician will assist in adding greater substance to the *arete* of freedom. When the helper is recognized, the freedom of existence without substantive order is overcome through the

---

[59] Eph. 1:7.   [60] Plato, *Republic*, 496.   [61] Aeschylus, *Agamemnon*, 160.
[62] Chesterton, Illustrated London News, January 14, 1911.

free community with Socrates; this is the movement from blindness to sight, from thinking one has sight as Oedipus did, to true sight which the blind Tiresias possessed and the blinded Oedipus outside of Colonus achieved. For this transcendent vision to occur, the false equality of dead souls – whether in Piraeus or Hades – is abolished.

In the dialogue, fate and free will receive a renewed articulation in the union of freedom and *arete* as orienting the hierarchical movement. Only when those two poles coalesce can the ascent be genuine, and not a false equality, the suffering of Orestes liberated only through the commission of justice in the *Eumenides* for the individual. Oedipus' self-imposed exile and sacrifice become the propaedeutic to *dike* as substitutional, taking on suffering for a selected few. Both these forms of justice are now expanded from the individual, the substitutional, to the civilizational, in the construction of the *polis*. Socrates is constructing the *polis* out of the Idea which is a "measureless toil," a wide scale *agon*. His ascent is hierarchy as listening: "the measure of listening to discourses of this kind is the whole life for wise man."[63] The charm of Socratic discourse is the resurrection of the soul from death to life with the savior/helper. Hierarchy is lost when human beings "do not mind their own business" and thus act like "lovers of opinion (*philodoxa*)." Such souls act out their existence without stable foundation, shifting between being and non-being. They constitute the equality of the lowest common denominator. This ascent only arrives at true equality in Christian monotheism, when we arrive at the sameness of transcendental experience shared in the body and blood of Christ as offer of individual substitutional, and civilizational justice. The danger of searching for this equality is that in anything else it becomes tyranny, as we see in the endless scapegoat mechanism of the Oresteia, and how quickly Creon becomes demonic in the Theban plays.[64] Searching for this strong theological basis which can offer Paradise has the danger of being immanentized and reducing life to tyranny, as Plato traces quite deftly in the *Republic*. We are looking for a true *epanados*, the ascent of the soul from the day that is actually night to the true day, and we need to be very sure of our guide, if we are to trust that fate can mingle into a positive freedom, and death truly issues life: "For we are

---

[63] Plato, *Republic*, 450b.

[64] Plato seeks the threshold where the expiation of ignorance through suffering is finally complete. But what *polis* can possibly overturn so much of the worldly ways? He may pay with his life and even then that is not enough. Cf. Plato, *Republic*, 343e: "And indeed, whenever either of them holds a position of authority, the just man, even if he suffers no other loss, suffers the deterioration of his personal affairs through neglect, and because he is just, he takes no personal advantage of public property, and besides all this, he is hated by his family and acquaintances when he is not prepared to afford them any service, beyond what is just. But what happens to the unjust man is the complete opposite of all this."

a fragrance of Christ to God among those who are being saved and among those who are perishing; to the one an aroma from death to death, to the other an aroma from life to life."[65]

The Resistance to death is central to civilizational formation, and its overcoming in the *apocalpysis* of the New Testament is the apex of what is sensed in the ascent from Piraeus, the ascent from Hades.

> And I saw the dead, great and small, standing before the throne, and books were opened. Another book was opened, which is the book of life. The dead were judged according to what they had done as recorded in the books. The sea gave up the dead that were in it, and death and Hades gave up the dead that were in them, and each person was judged according to what they had done. Then death and Hades were thrown into the lake of fire. The lake of fire is the second death. Anyone whose name was not found written in the book of life was thrown into the lake of fire.[66]

Philosophy and political thought have their roots in the resistance of the soul to its destruction by society, in the purgation of ignorance and guilt through painful illumination. This resistance forms the true society within the false society. This is a form of *epanados*. That which is *beyond* or transcends all experiences and thus encompassing all experiences can also be understood as *within* (immanence) all things. Being is beyond so to encompass all expressions because it is *within* all things. Society must be constructed on the relationship between the two, transcendence and immanence, orienting experience and ascent. Each human seeks the Good (*agathon*) because it is Transcendent beyond our worldly grasp and yet is immanent because each soul shares in its desire to seek out its nature and meaning. If we lose the transcendency of the Good, then society will find dangerous alternatives and false equalities, thinking that it is seeing, thinking that it is resisting death, but all the while blind and dying. Socrates notes that the philosopher comes first in civilization, protecting and upholding the relationship between immanence and transcendence. Then the sophist – the lover of opinion – follows him as the destroyer of his work through immanentization of the symbols of transcendence. Plato senses the startling demand of Christian monotheism: true humanity requires true theology; the person with a false theology is an untrue person. The person of *pseudos* has ignored divine meaning and made himself "god" through the drive of pleasures, power, money, and so on. He hides the truth. False equality steeps the soul in *pseudos*, in ignorance.

Truth, much like the turn away from false equality, turning away from the descent into Piraeus, requires a turning-around (*periagoge*) of the soul.

---

[65] 2. Cor. 2:15–16   [66] Rev. 20:12–15.

The restoration of the soul requires this turning away from *pseudos*, as Oedipus blinds himself in order to turn away from false sight.

The *Republic* has a clear martyrological dimension as key component of society, following in the footsteps of Oedipus' sacrifice, and foreshadowing Christ's ultimate overcoming of death through His death. We see this dimension in Socrates' stress that one man's actions diagnose the quality of a society: there are as many forms of government as there are men. "Must we not agree that in each of us there are the same forms and habits as in the *polis*? And from nowhere else do they pass there."[67] Philosophy is the anxious ascent toward salvation, to a paradisal society. The Philosopher has anxiety for himself and for others, for he understands himself in relation to others, fulfills his nature in relation to other. The ascent is Dionysian. It is an *eros*, a longing for a Transcendental meaning we cannot reach, but must reach. Because truth, *alethiological* meaning, is often veiled, the philosopher must keep vigil, this is also its own form of anxiety.

Plato understood political science as a two-fold act of spiritual resistance which conjures the powerhouse strong theology of Christian monotheism: (1) Salvation: the act of salvation for himself and others reconstitutes in himself and others the communal intelligibility to relieve the pressure of corruption; (2) Judgment: Since the *order* of the soul is recaptured in the resistance to the surrounding order this act illuminates the criteria for judgment of social order and disorder. This twofold order of salvation and judgment reaches its central identifying reality, its ultimate salvific helper – which Socrates prefigures – in Christ in the Gospels:

> "Lord," said Thomas, "we do not know where You are going, so how can we know the way?" Jesus answered, "I am the way and the truth and the life. No one comes to the Father except through Me. If you had known Me, you would know My Father as well. From now on you do know Him and have seen Him."[68]

Glaukon and Adeimantus demand to know what justice and injustice are "in themselves," because if a man knew that he would be his own "best guardian," for he would be *afraid* to enter communion with the greatest of evils" through unjust deeds.[69] Note the word "afraid," it returns us to our discussion of the virtue of anxiety. If we truly knew the Good, knew justice, we would be afraid to enter communion with evil by unjust acts. This fear rises as perfume of promise in Scripture. The awe for the divine is the salvific helper who can promise wisdom, knowing the true ascent to days multiplied, and life increased:

---

[67] Plato, *Republic*, 435e. [68] Jn. 14:5–7. [69] Cf. Plato, *Republic*, 366e–367a

> The fear of the Lord is the beginning of wisdom: And the knowledge of the
> holy is understanding. For by me thy days shall be multiplied, And the years
> of thy life shall be increased. If thou be wise, thou shalt be wise for thyself:
> But if thou scornest, thou alone shalt bear it.[70]

Plato's souls in fear of communion with evil, repelled by evil acts, call to mind
St. Paul's "submitting to one another in the fear of God"[71] as cornerstone of
religious community geared toward eternal life; fear as freedom and confidence,
yet another paradoxical tension within the shared poles of fate and freedom,
death, and life. The language of being "repelled" is important here, and critical
to the power of the salvific helper to pull us toward the Truth. Socrates'
blueprint for a Good Society is vastly separated from the language of the private
ideal of the Sophists. The Sophist is living out his own private desires, the
society of the opinion-based mindset can never rise to the communal because it
is not unified by what truly unifies human nature; instead, it is an abolishing of
transcendency. The Sophist – the liar and the corrupt – creates the "ideal" state
conjuring a dream, a fantasy, the construction of a social contract over and
against nature to enable each to act out their lowest common denominator
pleasures and whims. This is why the language of so many tyrannies is clear
immanentization and replacement of theological yearning for Paradise in the
Hegelian, Marxist, Hitlerian states. Each is an effort to immanentize transcendent categories such as truth, happiness, perfection, fulfillment, goodness,
beauty, and to overstep the strong theology of monotheism, creating false
utopias and worldly Paradises.

Plato is describing the *good polis*, the precursor to Paradise, not the *ideal
polis*, the precursor to tyranny and hell. The language of "ideal" turns into
"ideology." It is the act of supplanting a dreamlike value on existence and
demanding existence conform. Plato's city-state is not this. It is the effort to
reveal that the true society must seek to recover its imprint in the truth of the
divine which it obscures when freedom is not balanced with *arete*.[72]

Returning to our themes of descent and ascent, the good *polis* has two
directions, two poles, that must be held in the soul at all times, and stretched
into civilizational meaning, as the very backdrop of divinity.

1. The Experience of the Depth itself: the darkness, misery, despair, danger,
   evil in the depth of the false equality is only experienced *because* no matter
   how obscured the experience of the Good is, it is always in contrast.

---

[70] Prov. 9:10–12.   [71] Eph. 5:21.

[72] Words used to describe the good *polis* are concrete and grounded in the Real and thus the
transcendency is not dreamlike but truly the one and the many: "good" (434e/; 449a: 472e; 543c)
a "good in the full sense of the word (427e) "the best" (497e) "the best we can make" (434e) "the
best governed" (462d) "right" 449a) "eudaimonic/happy" (420b) "well ordered" (462e).

We know we are fallen *only* because we are already rising. Again, this is the experience of anxiety so key to the virtuous soul.

2. The Experience of a Direction from the Depth Upward: the fear of entering an evil community, being subsumed by it, of forgetting the good, the desire for the other, for salvation, for a "best guardian," to know not the appearance of the good but the good itself. All of this has the language of humility and thus the language of ascent. We are reminded of the Gospel of St. John: The *Logos* of God is the light of man that shines in the darkness and is not submerged by it.

The polis is man written at large. Government is thus the animation of the soul. Crucially, the soul of the leader stamps his soul on the institutions. The question of the formation and subsequent historical endurance of Christian monotheism is the soul of the leader, the salvific helper, the soul of Christ stamped large on society – Christ Who *Is* Heaven. With Francois Mauriac we can read a preliminary form of this traveler and guide in Socrates of the *Republic*:

> The Incarnation is the mystery of a God who travelled the entire road toward us, and who was not only one of us during His mortal life but has remained with us, and that is not all: He dwells within us. This being so, how could we aspire to find Him elsewhere if we possess Him here on Earth? I recall the Canticle of my First Communion: "Heaven has visited the Earth" ... Yes, and it has done more than visit the Earth, it has merged in it without annihilating itself, so that to die will be not only for us to leave the Earth but also to leave the Heaven we have possessed in the flesh even in the humiliation of sin and its tears.[73]

Why does Plato develop a paradigm for the right order of the *polis* if the good *polis* can be realized in the soul of the philosopher, and without his engaging in the hopeless task of reforming the corrupt society? This question is filled with meaning and points of interest. For one it shows us that while Plato's metaphysics of soul and body remain estranged, his body politique involves a union with soul and spirit that certainly overcomes the anthropology of the "prison house." Secondly, Plato is suggesting that the order of the psyche is practically absorbed by the pressures of the *polis*. We are communal beings, beings who find ourselves through otherness. This emphasis on the civilizational union as part of the individual soul, that there is a cosmic city to the soul, foreshadows the desire for the city of God in Paradise. Human existence for Plato meant political existence; and restoration of order in the soul implied the creation of a political order in which the restored citizen could exist as an active citizen. This is why the greatest achievement of the good soul is not escape from the corrupt society but finding just society in which to participate:

---

[73] Mauriac, *The Inner Presence*, 57.

> Yes, but not the greatest, since fortune has denied him the *politeia* to which he belongs; in that *politeia* he would grow to his fullness, and save not only his private but also the public weal. The Justice of the soul is more precious than participation in politics; and it must be purchased, if the circumstances are unfortunate, at the price of a diminution of human stature. The withdrawal of politics is heavy with resignation, for the fullness of growth, the maximal augmentation of man, can be achieved *only* through participation in the public life of the *polis*.[74]

This is foreshadowing again the City of God, the craving of Paradise wrought into Being by the singular salvific and martyrological figure, sensed in Oedipus, heightened in Socrates, dramatically embodied in the cosmic demand of Christ as fully God and fully Man. Does not Glaucon nascently touch on the power of a figure like Christ and of Paradise in the following remarks: "You mean the city whose establishment we have described, the city whose home is in the idea for I think that it can be found nowhere on earth."[75] This is yet again that *epanados*, that locus of atonement and expiation where fate can unite with freedom, freedom with *arete*, death with life. That Plato refused to separate the *polis* reflects our human nature and the realization that this nature may be seen and observed and kept in vigil by only a few.

The *polis* will only be a happy state if its architecture and its walls are designed "by painters who use the divine paradigm."[76] And these painters are "lovers of wisdom"[77] who, through their association with the divine order, have themselves become orderly and divine in the measure allowed to man. The strong monotheism which conjures paradisal hope and fulfillment is seen in the Philosopher King. The king is the one who sees farther and better, who can practice and enact political life more truly in the light of the sun, the salvific helper:

> Unless, said I, either philosophers become kings in our states or those whom we now call our kings and rulers take to the pursuit of philosophy seriously and adequately, and there is a conjunction of these two things, political power and philosophic intelligence, while the motley horde of the natures who at present pursue either apart from the other are compulsorily excluded, there can be no cessation of troubles, dear Glaucon, for our states, nor, I fancy, for the human race either. Nor, until this happens, will this constitution which we have been expounding in theory ever be put into practice within the limits of possibility and see the light of the sun.[78]

For the Philosopher King to rule, to guide us to what dominates our human nature but paradoxically does not manifest easily in daily life – yet another

---

[74] Plato, *Republic*, 497e, in Voegelin, *Order and History Vol. 3*, 144–45.

[75] Plato, *Republic*, 592a–b.   [76] Plato, *Republic*, 500e.   [77] Plato, *Republic*, 500 c–d.

[78] Plato, *Republic*, 473 c–d.

pole of tension – the leader must utilize the *gennaion*, the big or noble lie which alone can convey the truth.[79] The founders have agreed on a falsehood, the Phoenician Tale, as the origin of their *polis*. Is this problematic or does it underscore a deeper truth? Is it a mythos or is it a lie? Is it a story that reflects what's transcendently true but not empirically true? Is this why all monotheistic power functions on martyrological acts, so that persons unite in hope of salvation and paradise in the transcendentally true reality, but a reality not reflected in the empirical truths?

The founders of the *polis* will tell its citizens the Phoenician Tale to persuade subtly to be guided by transcendent truth. First, they must convince the rulers and the soldiers, as they cannot turn against the society and have the most power to do so, and then the rest of the citizens, that all their training, education which separates them into *this* or *that* specialty was imagined in a dream. In truth, during that time they all had been under the earth, including their weapons and other equipment which were being shaped and prepared. When they were finished, the earth as their mother delivered them so that they could take their respective places and defend their land as their mother had brought them forth to do. In this case, each must regard the other as his brother or sister, all of the same earth. Think here of "ashes to ashes and dust to dust," we are born of ashes and ashes we will return. This is what unites us in hope for Resurrection to eternal paradisal life:

> Forasmuch as it hath pleased Almighty God of his great mercy to take unto himself the soul of our dear brother here departed: we therefore commit his body to the ground; earth to earth, ashes to ashes, dust to dust; in sure and certain hope of the Resurrection to eternal life, through our Lord Jesus Christ; who shall change our vile body, that it may be like unto his glorious body, according to the mighty working, whereby he is able to subdue all things to himself.[80]

When each was completed and born to the earth the god then fashioned some as rulers and mixed gold into their race, and some were helpers and soldiers and he mixed silver into their race, and some were farmers and craftsman and he mixed iron and brass into their race, but all are of the earth as brothers and sisters each helping the other out. Now races would intermingle and thus a silver father may have a gold child and so forth, so it was the command of the god of the rules to sort out the children so that a brass/craftsman was not a soldier, or a ruler and a silver was not confused as a brass or gold, and so on. The *polis* will perish if the brass rule, if we are not in our proper place. If disorder flourishes, the *polis* will degenerate. It is one thing to *say* we are equal, but the conceptual recognition of equality does not have the power to impart the unity, the brotherhood needed for the hierarchical ascent to truth in

---

[79] Plato, *Republic*, 414c.   [80] *The Book of Common Prayer*, 577.

the *polis* to function. The noble lie which is really transcendent truth reminds us of St. Paul on charismata, spiritual gifts. St. Paul stresses a similar point in terms of the gold, silver, and brass and yet urges the universal brotherhood. St. Paul first distinguishes the charismata and their function in the community, and the importance of utilizing those charismata in the proper place and their function in the community, and then reminds Christians that, in spite their different endowments, they still are all members of the one body of Christ *sternly* and that the most devoted service is worthless unless formed to love. We see this also in Galatians:

> So in Christ Jesus you are all children of God through faith, for all of you who were baptized into Christ have clothed yourselves with Christ. There is neither Jew nor Gentile, neither slave nor free, nor is there male and female, for you are all one in Christ Jesus. If you belong to Christ, then you are Abraham's seed, and heirs according to the promise.[81]

Socrates the Physician sees the differences and the endowments in a manner like St. Paul. The "lie" that may be the truth points us to a prime Socratic truth. No empirical data (i.e., income, job, advancement, wealth) will show us the equality among men, no empirical data will convince us of the brotherhood among strangers. This common humanity must be unified within that shared transcendence. Any other exterior or forceful form of generic unity, by immanentizing transcendence in communism, tyranny, fascism, democracies, cannot unite us but more often suppresses and perverts the soul. This is a startling foreshadowing of Christian community enshrining hope for the equality which only Paradise can provide. Socrates is dramatically searching for the experience of family to be extended beyond family lines. If the different gifts (divisions of gold, silver, brass) are dreams compared to the brotherhood, this familial unity is essential to stymie evil pride that may take possession of rulers or may cause dissension among workers. Pride functions when it takes on the character of "truth," when the divisions seem more real than the brotherhood. This must be understood as a falling away from the truth. The big lie is subtly transformed into the Great Truth: equality can only be conceived spiritually, but spiritual vision takes time, it is the last thing ever seen and only with great effort. Plato is leading us to the totalizing purgation of ignorance, evil, and lies through affliction even unto death.[82]

---

[81] Gal. 3:26.

[82] Plato is leading us towards this expiation but also failing in the process. His project in the *Republic* rooted in strong position to the tyrannical unreality but veers towards it. Plato's sense of *lysis* subtly acknowledges that he lacks a certain revelatory structure that would harmonize all the opposing tensions of existence. In Christianity, all Salvation is the holding together of opposing poles that

Again, while Plato's metaphysics holds a separation between the soul and body so much so that the soul's entrapment in the body prevents the soul from realizing its true nature, it is interesting to note that the soul of the *polis* is now heavily linked to the body, to the concrete, to the communal and the familial. Plato is attempting to create a family unity which overcomes the disruptive family divides and warring factions. His thoughts were a precursor to the Neoplatonic idea of a spiritual community united by the *Agathon*, by God as Goodness in Christian communities where each person is brother or sister. This is why Plato's thought has been instrumental in the formation of religious communities. He sees the corrupted forms of *polis* ultimately *disembodied*. The persons ruling have no sense of familial tie except to their own and ultimately that is dwindled down only to their own ego.

How then does a good *polis* built on a stable enduring order move out of its stable order? Plato points to the instability of the cosmic form itself. This is a metaphysical and theological insight which dramatically yearns for the strong theology of Christian monotheism revealed in Christ as Paradisal promise fulfilled. Plato, appealing to Homer, states that what has been born must perish. The good *polis*, *because* built on the image and likeness of the Good, appears unshakeable, but because it is built in time, must suffer *lysis* (dissolution).

Everything in existence points to these changing tides, to this instability, to this inability to find a perfect form. All creatures, plants, and animals, have periods of fertility and infertility both of soul and body. The wisest of rulers will in time miss his mark, the Guardians will miscalculate the right time for action, unions between two people will not be done for the best reasons, and so on. Again, we see the analogy of the gold, silver and brass or iron souls raised. Somewhere in all of this the rise of the ego will inevitably manifest. This dissension will bring about small but growing egoisms, a drive for power or money as a reflection of the self, or the family, and so on. From here Plato traces the transitions into corrupted city-states – oligarchy, timocracy, democracy, and tyranny. The good *polis* is not exempt from the cosmic mystery of Being and Becoming: the form that has been embodied will be disembodied. It will lose its true self, its concreteness, its lifeforce within and related to the *Agathon*.

Crucially and suggestively, Plato admits that it is beyond the powers of man to overcome the transitory nature of existence. We cannot overcome the becoming/flux to create a *polis* as stable and eternal as eternal Being *Itself*. The Good

---

must come together but we have no power to unite them. A mortal woman gave life to God, Christ is fully God and fully man, and death is the way to life. How can we believe it all to be possible? But we must believe. It is necessary for our eternal life and happiness.

polis is an instantiation, an image of the eternal form in becoming a fleeting moment between creation and dissolution. The Good *polis* captures the moment when the thrown ball is neither rising nor falling. Additionally, and also filled with nuance foreshadowing the strong theology of the Christ event: the failure of the good *polis* is not a mere historical event that somehow could have been avoided by human hands and decision. Again, we shall see that this failure isn't an historical event; it isn't something that can be prevented or corrected by temporal measures. For Plato, it is the failure to maintain the mythical incarnation of the Love of the Good in a world of Becoming. Even though we see these failings throughout time, it is not within human power and temporality to correct. The "sequence" of Perilous Political Forms: timocracy, oligarchy, democracy, tyranny. These are the corruptive stages through which the good and true *polis*, built as a reflection of eternal Being, slips down on its way to decline to the "ultimate malady of the *polis*."[83]

The collapse of the *polis* is not a mere historical event but a metaphysical reflection of human nature in relation to the divine. The source of the failing to maintain the incarnation of the good *polis* is not reducible to an historical event, time, or place but rooted in the very nature of human existence – that we seek the eternal in a temporal world. Here, yet again, we are witnessing how one pole of tensions calls to mind another, as fate calls out freedom in Oedipus blinding himself, and death calls out eternal life in the dying God, the failure of the good *polis*[84] calls forth the desire for the City of God, the Paradise community that does not fail.

> Perhaps in that kingdom we shall see on the bodies of the Martyrs the traces of the wounds which they bore for Christ's name: because it will not be a deformity, but a dignity in them; and a certain kind of beauty will shine in them, in the body, though not of the body.[85]

Plato in the *Republic* teaches us that empirical ordering will fail, that we need *mythos* to provide spiritual as political unity. If Plato sees the descent of the soul as the corresponding disintegration of the *polis*, and this is built on the inability to retain the good, no amount of empirical observation can build a good society. For Plato, one must recover the *mythos*, the "noble lie" which is the truth beyond empirical sight, the mystical union of all souls which can order the *polis*. But it

---

[83] Plato, *Republic*, 544c.

[84] Cf. Plato, *Apology*, 38e–39a: "Neither in war nor yet at law ought any man to use every way of escaping death. For often in battle there is no doubt that if a man will throw away his arms, and fall on his knees before his pursuers, he may escape death; and in other dangers there are other ways of escaping death, if a man is willing to say and do anything. The difficulty, my friends, is not in avoiding death, but in avoiding unrighteousness; for that runs faster than death."

[85] St. Augustine, *The City of God*, xxii.

will become disembodied again; the good *polis* cannot maintain itself forever. There is no human power that can assure its permanence. The hunger for transcendence in the *Republic* can only be met in the Paradisal promise of a strong monotheism. In the Allegory of the Cave: "The good is the last thing ever seen and only with effort"[86] so that ordering a society by empirical observations, by a generalization of institutional phenomena, from the past and present, will not be sufficient to create the good *polis*.

A strong monotheism can only assure us of Paradise if it resides beyond empiricism and historical event. If, for example, the death of Christ was merely an historical, empirical event happening over 2,000 years ago how is the death of one man on a Cross a civilizational point of unity when there are innumerable men and women throughout time who have died in similar fashion and circumstances? If the story of Christ is only passed on by *mimesis* and a tradition of *mimesis*, why not call Christ any other person who has died in similar circumstances? But if the story is truly the carrier of *mythos*, it is then a transcendent reality beyond all expression. *Mythos* is not a lie but the carrier of primal truth. Plato is searching for the *mythos* of all myths which can assure the permanence of the good society, make Paradise real not ideal and false. In the fulfillment of *Mythos*,[87] each Good Friday *is* Good Friday. In Christ we are not merely recognizing an anniversary of a past event but experiencing *periagoge* (turnaround). We are turning around and re-collecting what truly *Is*.[88] We see a glimpse of this reality in Plato. The good *polis* always exists before the corrupted ones. While Plato argues against the idea that the fallen political forms follow an inevitable historical or empirical order – timocracy will not

---

[86] Plato, *Republic*, 517b.

[87] *Mythos* is the underlying interpretive foundation we carry with us; it links events within the titanic wave of life and experience that precedes and permeates our historical beings within the deposit of the faith. Cf. Holman, "Mythos and History: A Review of Matthew Boulter's 'Repetition and Mythos: Ratzinger's Bonaventure and the Meaning of History'." *Mythos* helps us to "navigate between the Scylla of reactionary traditionalism and the Charybdis of exuberant thirteenth-century autonomous scientism … any 'rational' discourse had to unfold within the sapiential framework of the life of faith as envisioned by the Church. The cold facts of logical reasoning needed an interpretive framework if they were to contribute to the flourishing existence of the whole human person … [*Mythos*] is a 'middle way' between the abstract universality of Aristotle's *theoria* and the particular facts of historical events. Only through the illumination of the existential desire of the whole person made possible by a comprehensive *mythos* can history be assigned any real meaning."

[88] Cf. Ratzinger, *Eschatology*, 223: "God himself suffered and died … He himself entered into the distinctive freedom of sinners, but he went beyond it in that freedom of his own love which descended willingly into the Abyss. Here the real quality of evil and its consequences become quite palpable, provoking the question … whether in this event we are not in touch with a divine response able to draw freedom, precisely as freedom, to itself. The answer lies hidden in Jesus' descent into Sheol, in the night of the soul which he suffered, a night no one can observe except by entering this darkness in suffering faith."

necessarily lead to oligarchy, and so on – he does note that the good *polis* in its many forms will *always* precede corrupted forms. This is an important metaphysical point: evil, corruption, imperfections depend upon a source, and they cannot truly be themselves. They require the good which they violate for their existence. For Plato, the loss of *mythos* in culture is devastating. But if there is to be a *mythos*, it must be True; *mythos* cannot merely degenerate into an art as personal expression (*mimesis*), it must be transcendental.

Socrates sees that the age of myth has died, and he is searching to recover it in the dialogue, for myth once united us and formed the Good *polis*. He is now looking for Philosophy to take the place of Myth. Perhaps it is not Philosophy but Revelation. Does the Christ event accomplish this reality? Its enduring promise of Paradise seems to complete what Plato desired in the *Phoenician Tale*. Here resides the issue: How do you tell this scientific culture that the myth that all humans come from the same earth – the Phoenician tale – must be believed. They are no longer apt to hear or to believe it. Their inability to hear it is not necessarily an advancement for Plato. And thus what *will* unite them? This is Plato's search. Plato's desire predates the Christ event and yet has a beautiful symmetry with it. His search for the prime *mythos* that carries the truth has a vastly suggestive element to it. Plato is looking for something that surpasses *mythos*. Whereas the myth degenerates in time to an old wives tale, something to look at or more often than not look down upon, he is looking for the mythos that begins and never leaves its source, "its original artist."[89] The soul for Plato is immortal, while grain will mildew, wood will rot and the body of man will wither through disease and old age, the soul is not destroyed by its own evils or the evils of another. When the soul lives by temporality, temporal pleasures, it will, by condition, become sick. Only when the soul considers itself in its proper immortality can its nature as divine be revealed and through it the cultivation of a proper *paideia* and political life. Only when we yearn for our company in the eternal can we act out justice properly: "The soul ought to do what is just, whether it possesses a ring of Gyges or not."[90] Our true life is always in reference to the divine, for our souls are eternal. If we live following only after pragmatic and temporal goods and pleasures to the *suppression* of the eternal and enduring good, we cannot be happy. We are only happy when we are like gods, which is not possible through a tyrannical eros which is only the accumulation of goods which *will* fail, which *will* rot and *will* die out.

We are rewarded in this life for good actions *because* we are living according to the true nature of our souls as eternal and divine. There may not be empirical evidence for these rewards but Plato never placed much weight on

---

[89] Plato, *Republic*, 607a.   [90] Plato, *Republic*, 612b.

that empirical evidence. This is the risk and a crucial cornerstone of the dialogue, and crucial to Christian monotheism, where the evidence for all our Paradisal hope is not found on earth filled with disease, inequality, injustice, and death.

> When evening came, the owner of the vineyard said to his foreman, "Call the workers and pay them their wages, beginning with the last ones hired and going on to the first." The workers who were hired about five in the afternoon came and each received a denarius. So when those came who were hired first, they expected to receive more. But each one of them also received a denarius. When they received it, they began to grumble against the landowner. "These who were hired last worked only one hour," they said, "and you have made them equal to us who have borne the burden of the work and the heat of the day." But he answered one of them, "I am not being unfair to you, friend. Didn't you agree to work for a denarius? Take your pay and go. I want to give the one who was hired last the same as I gave you. Don't I have the right to do what I want with my own money? Or are you envious because I am generous?" "So the last will be first, and the first will be last."[91]

In closing this section, do we not see Aristotle struggling with something akin to paradisal demands in the predicament of human immortality in relationship to the body? Aristotle's own difficulty of isolating the immortal element of the soul continues this interrogative precursor to the hope for Paradise we see in Plato's *Republic*. Each, from differing poles of the relationship of body and soul and civilizational formation, is circling the ecstatically revealed Christian monotheism which necessitates the God-Man, and audaciously claims Paradise in the Resurrected state. In the questions on happiness and friendship in *Nicomachean Ethics* humans may desire immortality but not accomplish it. That which is impossible may be an object of hope but not of choice or power. The rather enigmatic remarks in Book VIII, where exemplary and divine-like friendship is yearned for but unable to be found, place us within the captivating urgency and centrality of Paradise within humanity.

But such a life would be too high for man; for it is not insofar as he is man that he will live so, but in so far as something divine is present within him; and by so much as this is superior to our composite nature is its activity superior to that which is the exercise of the other kind of virtue. If reason is divine, then, in comparison with man, the life according to it is divine in comparison with human life. But we must not follow those who advise us, being men, to think of human things, and, being mortal, of mortal things, but must, so far as we can, make ourselves immortal, and strain every nerve to live in accordance with the

---

[91] Mt. 20:8–16.

Figure 3 Chalices Burning.JPG, by Carol Scott

best thing in us; for even if it be small in bulk, much more does it in power and worth surpass everything.[92]

4 Holiness and Violence: A Christian View of the Resurrected State

> But our citizenship is in heaven, and from it we await a Savior, the Lord Jesus Christ, who will transform our lowly body to be like his glorious body, by the power that enables him even to subject all things to himself.
>
> – Philippians[93]

The preceding sections have exposed tension regarding *why* the possibility of the afterlife, as the overcoming of suffering and the completion of happiness, emphasizes a singularity, a unity, a central figure as Law, Fate, Wisdom, and Expiator.[94] Now we must touch on the wreckage death enacts on the unity of body and soul. The price of admission for Paradise in a monotheistic structure appears too high to pay. Existential violence has underscored our discussion so far, whether viewed from the sheer immanence of the tragedians, where the gods are too close, or the conceptual impossibility of the philosophers, where the distance between God and Man is protracted over the aeons. In this final section, the annihilating power of abnegation and abandonment are revealed as the core movement of Monotheism and Paradise. Some *one* person must carry all these tensions and sublimate them if Paradise is to be realized; it must be won

---

[92] Aristotle, *Nicomachean Ethics*, 1177b27–1178a10.   [93] Phil. 3:20–21.

[94] Cf. 1 John 2:2: "He himself is the sacrifice that atones for our sins – and not only our sins but the sins of all the world."

through flesh and blood. God must become Man; the city of man must give way to the city of God.[95] This section will conclude by exploring the structural mystery of Christ as fully God and fully man, giving a limited but careful accounting of why the mystery of the hypostatic union provides the only access to Paradise befitting the human person's embodied nature. What is understood from the tragedians to Plato is that embodiment, woundedness, death have been both central to and the stumbling block to Paradisal completion.

Christ is the heart and completion of a robust, specified, strong theology in which His Being *is* the way. He is apex and estuary of all human-and-divine desire for the invisible to be made visible and tangibly present in the Flesh as one with Spirit. The God-Man is a dual unity, not a dualism of unrelated natures held together by forced dialogue and strained connections. There can be no dividing line cut down the middle of Christ, no partition of the curtain, when convenient, that distinguishes His intellectual and embodied experiences, some pertaining to God and others pertaining to Man. Either His soul is the form of His body, or it is not. Either Christ is fully man and fully God, or the whole desire for the Resurrected State is grounded on lamentably faulty foundations. Paradise, in this highest of monotheisms, is a gamble, everything is at stake.

What weak theology rightfully rejects uninformative bifurcations and naïve dualisms, but in its rejection, it sidesteps the essential.[96] The dual unity of the God-Man alone recovers and renews, with exacting precision, what is lost in the violent separation of body and soul. Weak theology vacates the transcendent power of a real irreducible divine ontological otherness. It mutes the maddening yearning for Heaven as the only satisfying end. No vague term or modernist parable of love or justice or humanity can satisfy this desire. Christ speaks in parables because the end is not yet unveiled for us, but it has never been the product of our world-forming. There is within us a very real duality of the world and heaven, of death and eternal life. It does not take a trained metaphysician to sense that through death, the soul is cleaved

---

[95] This singular figure must break the cycle of non-redemptive violence. The God-Man alone can give through his body and blood the expiation of our guilt through suffering. Only then in the opening of his wounds do we enter Heaven. Cf. Girard, *I See Satan Falling Like Lightning*, 122: "The Christian passion is not anti-Jewish, as the vulgar antisemites believe; it is anti-pagan; it reinterprets religious violence in such a negative fashion as to make its perpetrators feel guilty for committing it, even for silently accepting it. Since all human culture is grounded in this collective violence, the whole human race is declared guilty from the standpoint of the Gospels. Life itself is slandered because life cannot continue and organize itself without this type of violence."

[96] Caputo, *After the Death of God*, 82: "I do not distinguish between two different worlds but two different logics, the logic of the mundane constituted economies and the logic of the event that disturbs them, and I see in Jesus of Nazareth an exemplary embodiment of the logic or paralogic of the gift, who told paradoxical parables about and who was himself a paradoxical parable of the kingdom of God, which he opposed to the economy of the 'world'."

unnaturally from the body, that a torn and ruptured occurrence in the heart of Being has marked and re-marked the face of the earth. While we must be attentive to the false divisions, we must also be careful not to miss the genuine dual intensity of body and soul that characterizes a human life and, at its core, houses our desire for Heaven

4.1 Monotheism and the Disconcerting State of the Separated Soul

Believe with Saint Thomas that the intellectual incompleteness of the human soul needs the body in order to become an intellectual whole, and you are forced to believe both that the unity of human nature is intellectual and that death is – may I say it – an offense against that unity ... Why should Saint Thomas have said that for the soul of man to be separated from its body is against its nature, unless the human essence requires both body and soul for the constitution of that essence? What is death then? Is it simply a separation of the soul from the body, or is it the breakup of the human essence? On purely philosophical grounds, Saint Thomas stands in the way of conceding the second alternative, and the question is to know how to understand this formidable philosophical fact. Indeed, we seem to be in a dilemma. We cannot deny death as a fact of nature, but neither can we deny that, in constituting the human essence, soul and body belong together. They belong so much so that the Saint Thomas who said that it was against the nature of the soul to be without the body has also said that the separated soul was, according to its nature, in an unnatural condition. Thus, the more we see immortality and death in the light of the unity of man's nature, the more we wonder what to say about either one. Can we simply let the parts of human nature go their respective ways? Saint Thomas the metaphysician is saying we cannot. Immortality, even when it involves the separation of the soul from the body, cannot include that separation as part of its meaning. After all, what is an immortality that includes an unnatural condition? And what can we say about the death of the body, even if it be called a natural event in the world of bodies, if that death is against the nature of the soul and therefore the economy of the human essence? Admit the unity of human nature, therefore, as Saint Thomas conceives it, and you cannot think of either the death of the body or the separation of the soul from the body as natural.

– Anton Pegis, "St. Thomas and the Meaning of Human Existence"[97]

So far, we have uncovered and traced aspects of a monotheistic structure, whereby a strong singular divine figure – as fulcrum for the expiation of guilt, the fulfillment of justice – has the transcendent and metaphysical power to assure Paradise. We saw this burgeoning monotheistic God in diverse forms in the Pre-Socratics, where each thinker we discussed is seeking to isolate the underlying source which can be the nucleus of what *IS*, can be the *arche* and *telos*. When we turned to Aeschylus and Sophocles, we approached the

---

[97] Pegis, "St. Thomas and the Meaning of Human Existence," 63.

intrusion of the gods in human affairs as a sorting out of the key cosmogonic polarity and tension which indelibly marks all human life – fate and free will. What source can possibly guarantee that both coexist and are fulfilled in the other? This pole of tension is then raised in Plato as it is seen in the companion dialogic drama of soul and body, mortality and immortality, the natural and supernatural, truth and *Gennaion*. All these tensions need an apex, a point of origin and transformative holy violence, where they are resolved. We see this need in Plato's own admission that *lysis* prevents any Good *polis* from perpetual endurance; it will always break down and degenerate. The Good *polis* is a foreshadowing of the City of God, of Paradise. Unlike Paradise, it is a glimpse, the moment when the thrown ball is at its highest and has not yet dropped. Such a moment in history is brief, fleeting, and rarely experienced, but when it is sensed, it cultivates in the soul the wisdom of, and totalizing desire for, the beyond: the goal of something like Christian Paradise that we see in Plato. The question of strong monotheism hits its central identity issue *and* stumbling block in the problem of death, in the unnatural separation of soul and body. Both the foundation for the hope of Paradise as well as a disintegrating sense of Paradise are working as poles of tension within Christian monotheism. Paradoxically, the separation of the body and soul prompt the desire for Paradise and mute that desire as well, for humans cannot understand, imagine, or desire a disembodied state. This is the predicament at the core of Christian belief: Paradise is the central goal and yet often a vacant one, the structure of belief in *all* oriented toward Heaven and yet Heaven fails to be envisioned, fleshed out. We seek a vibrant resurrect state in which, with St. Bernard, we are "completely engulfed in that immense ocean of eternal light and everlasting brightness."[98]

The loss of a desire for Paradise comes from a degraded sense of Heaven as *beyond*. This beyondness of Heaven is misconceived to mean that it should be

---

[98] St. Bernard, "On Loving God," *Selected Works* n. 30: "But what about those souls which are already separated from their bodies? We believe they are completely engulfed in that immense ocean of eternal light and everlasting brightness. But if, which is not denied, they wish that they had received their bodies back or certainly if they desire and hope to receive them, there is no doubt that they have not altogether turned from themselves, for it is clear they still cling to something of their own to which their desires return though ever so slightly. Consequently, until death is swallowed up in victory and eternal light invades from all sides the limits of night and takes possession to the extent that heavenly glory shines in their bodies, souls cannot set themselves aside and pass into God. They are still attached to their bodies, if not by life and feeling, certainly by a natural affection, so that they do not wish nor are they able to realize their consummation without them. This rapture of the soul, which is its most perfect and highest state, cannot, therefore, take place before the resurrection of the bodies, lest the spirit, if it could reach perfection without the body, would no longer desire to be united to the flesh. For indeed, the body is not deposed or resumed without profit for the soul . . . . How true that text is which says that all things turn to the good of those who love God. [Rom 8,28] The sick, dead and resurrected body is a help to the soul who loves God; the first for the fruits of penance, the second for repose, and the third for consummation. Truly the soul does not want to be perfected, without that from whose good services it feels it has benefitted by in every way."

left un-wrestled with and uncontemplated. It is the predicament and folly of Christian monotheism that the strong singular divine figure that can metaphysically assure us of Paradise is emphasized, while Paradise itself is left unexamined. When these two realities are held together the contrast is almost unbearable, calling into question the Christian vision. We see how this under emphasized Paradise begins in in the afterthought view of the Resurrection, in its weak theological vision. Here the radicality of the Incarnation and Christ's rescue mission ends with a whimper rather than a bang. When God becomes a specter, a ghostly event, a whisper at night behind our backs, what else is there then for it soon to be an undernourished pliable idea of justice or forgiveness.

> The question is, when it comes to defining the scene of the crucifixion, how Christian we are willing to be and how radical our theology of the Cross will be. How genuinely, how seriously are we to take this central Christian vision? Is Jesus really unable to come down from the cross, or does he only seem to be (*dokein*)? ... If the kingdom Jesus preached were a kingdom of real power, he could, by a mighty roar – nay better, by a soft word – from his mouth spring the nails from his hands, thrust away the speaks from the hands of the soldiers, heal the wounds of his flesh, and shatter the cross into a million splinters in a dazzling display of sheer might ... But in the powerlessness of that death the word of God rose up in majesty as a word of contradiction, as the Spirit of God, as a specter, as a ghostly event that haunts us, but not a spectacular presence.[99]

Why is the hope for Paradise downgraded to a realm "out-there" and unknown, an unspectacular ghostly presence? What has transpired for this to occur? The human situation is that we are preoccupied with, while at the same time ignoring the Pauline injunction: "For this world is not our permanent home; we are looking forward to a home yet to come."[100] In essence, we speak of paradise at the deathbed, in our anxieties, at the funeral, it dominates those events, but it's a fearful speaking that does not venture much beyond the utterance itself – the "better place," or the "resting in peace," or the "with the angels now." How then does this odd simultaneity of preoccupation and neglect transpire historically? Much has to do with the state of the separated soul. In the *Suma Contra Gentiles*, St. Thomas remarks:

> For the human soul is immortal, and continues after its separation from the body. Yet union with body is essential to it, for by its very nature soul is form of body. Without body it is in an unnatural condition; and what is unnatural cannot go on forever. Therefore the soul, which is perpetual, is not for ever apart from the body, but will be united with it. The soul's immortality, therefore, seems to demand the eventual Resurrection of body.[101]

---

[99] Caputo, *The Weakness of God*, 43–44.   [100] Heb. 13–14.
[101] St. Thomas, *Summa Contra Gentiles*, 4, 79.

The monotheistic vision of death overcome in Paradise carries all those polarities to the point that we get to the drama and difficulty of the separated soul. This is the core tension of a strong singular divinity, but it has the danger of an emptied reality, an anti-phenomenological state rather than one reflective of lived experience, of the union of body and soul. For Aquinas, the soul is the form of the body, and the body fulfills the operations of the soul. Their co-part essential unity is one of mutual transcendence. The human person strains to imagine a disembodied heaven which is akin to imagining running without legs, or seeing without eyes, or breathing without lungs and circulatory system. Not only is the beyondness of heaven situated in the transcendence of its properties, but the beyondness also problematically conjures incredulity, an inability to square the circle. The soul is the form of the body, in Heaven we lack our bodies how then is Heaven a place of paradise without our intrinsic co-part?

The state of the separated soul is the prime crisis of a strong monotheism. In question 90, the objector attempts to square the circle stating that the soul must be *only* what God intended to be lasting by arguing that the human soul was created before its body therefore it is proportional that it outlasts the body.[102] Aquinas' response invokes the predicament of Christian monotheism – we seek Paradise, we seek the Resurrected state because our human nature as body and soul, the body *for* the soul and the soul *for* the body, and there cannot be paradise if our human nature is bypassed or truncated. He also reminds us that the soul outlasts is only due to the defects to the body caused by original sin."[103]

Additionally, if the soul is not only *for* the body, but the *body* fulfills the tools of the soul, one may rightly wonder what kind of knowledge, if any, the soul has in an unnatural state of separation? Aquinas goes to great lengths to address how the separated soul can still know in heaven. If the body provides our turning to phantasms essential to knowledge, how can the separated soul provide what it lacks?[104] The body and soul are not an accidental union which can be easily cleaved apart; vast spiritual violence occurs in that separation and estrangement, foreshadowed in all the previous dialogic tensions, particularly fate and free will. It takes a powerful singular divinity, the commanding promise of monotheism, to lay the groundwork for Paradise, particularly when most understand, at least latently, that a heaven perpetually estranged from embodiment is no heaven at all.

St. Thomas sets out to demonstrate how the soul is the highest of embodied beings but the lowest of intellectual substances. Still, we are closer to angels than to animals, and have the capacity to be knowingly receptive to the divine

---

[102] Cf. ST I, 90, 4, obj. 3.   [103] Cf. ST I, 90, 4 ad. 3.   [104] Cf. ST I, 89, 1 *resp.*

light. Angelic knowledge is nobler than the human turn to phantasms. Angels receive knowledge by turning to the intelligible object itself. Bypassing the phantasms is befitting an angel, but it does not befit a human soul which is supposed to be housed in carnality. Any advocacy for angelism would render the body an accident, an inessential addition to the soul, downgrading human dignity, embodiment, and the world of experience. If Paradise amounted to a form of knowledge equivalent to the angels' direct turning to the spiritual substance, then we would be in an existential impasse: Paradise would not be a state of perfection befitting human nature. And it would be nonsense for Paradise to be a state void of knowledge, as this also fails to reflect human nature. All along, the strong monotheism which offers Paradise has walked a conceptual and existential tightrope. Therefore, the promise of monotheism is Paradise fleshed out in the hope for the Resurrection; it is the audacity that God takes on dramatic impossibilities of life and renders them possible – fate leads to freedom, death leads to life, the loss of the body leads to the recovery of a glorified body.

Aquinas seeks to reconcile this difficulty by recognizing that the state of the separated soul of the blessed is *also* in a paradoxical polarity: it is a concession due to original sin but also denotes a nobler state, with no lacking whatsoever. God, in His mercy, acts in place of the phantasms and, because He is Being itself, He can authentically take this position for His creatures, without violating their epistemological nature. If the concession were not respected then Aquinas would be sidestepping the tensions of existence that we have seen from the Pre-Socratics, through the Tragedians and in Plato's struggle to understand *lysis* in the good *polis*. But if Paradise denotes lacking, then God would not be *esse ipsum subsistens*, in which all perfections are identical to Him and ever directed toward Him, and strong monotheism would fall into contradiction.

4.2 Christ as Paradise: Concluding Remarks

"The Beauty of God is the cause of the being of all that is."[105] To see the ancient Transcendentals elevated, to experience the existential poles of tension united, is to acknowledge that something or, rather someone – Christ – is their embodied eternal fulfillment. Christ's incarnation is the estuary of fate and free will at their union. His salvific act is both entirely necessary and utterly gratuitous. He marries death and eternal life, the maximum of carnality and spirituality, nature and super-nature, the terminus of the pre-Socratic struggle with immanence and transcendence. Christ fulfills the contradictory but

---

[105] St. Thomas, *In Librum Beati*, IV.

civilizational impulse that death brings life. His *beyond* goodness perfection and beauty renders that He *cannot* be too good to be true, but is instead too good *not* to be true. This is the interweaving logic of Christian monotheism brought to it fulcrum in Christ *as* Paradise.

One could characterize this unity of the transcendentals as the legitimate hermeneutic or logic of perfection in which it would not be possible for Christ to be on the one hand *too good* and on the other *not true*. Christ is the realization of the abstract first principles *as embodied*.[106] Christ is the truth not as idea but as person. He is existence not as unsaid facticity but Word made flesh. The first principles, by which all of existence have gathered momentum within the strong singular divine figure, is realized in Christ Who carries all existential poles within His unified being. The promise of Paradise, its legitimacy, rests on Christ's capacity to endure and survive – even unto death – these poles of seeming contradiction. In essence, the belief in Paradise in monotheism rests on the very wounds of Christ:

> "Behold I have gaven you on the palm of my hands." Who could wipe away what God has gaven on his hands? The hands of the glorious body of Christ bear forever the scars (*stigmates*) of the unforgettable, as the eternal memorial of time and history. The unforgettable that we watch for and watch over is founded in an unforgettable for God and by God himself. Its source is found in the unhoped for.[107]

Belief in Paradise hinges on the singular force of Christ, resolved in His resurrected scars. This is the astonishing foundation in which Word and Act, fate and free will, necessity and grace, immanence and transcendence, eternity and time, death and life, unite in the image of Christ. Christ's supreme gift on the Cross is the atonement of our guilt and sin through suffering. This is what is sensed by blinded Oedipus and in Plato's uneasy view of Paradise. But without Christ it is unable to be fulfilled, for no human can undo death, and put back together what cannot be separated, the body and soul. When attempted, it is done by reduction and denial, or a reconfiguring of priorities or a redefinition of terms as seen in a weak theology, but never faced head on in the burning truth of the *agon*. Our expiation needed the strongest of theological power to *become* the littleness of broken humanity.[108] God became man and consumed the wrath of

---

[106] Cf. St. Thomas, *De Veritate*, XI: "Now the light of reason by which [self-evident] principles are evident to us is implanted in us by God as a kind of reflected likeness in us of the uncreated truth. So, since human teaching can be effective only in virtue of that light, it is obvious that God alone teaches interiorly and principally, just as nature alone heals interiorly and principally."

[107] Chrétien, *The Unforgettable*, 98.

[108] Cf. Balthasar, *Theo-logic II*, 288: "We can speak of a depositing, a dimming, a non-use of his divine vision; his prayer must spring from his having become man."

God. Our inability to suffer enough to recover love is now covered by Christ's sacrifice.[109] We are ransomed from death.

> God presented Christ as a sacrifice of atonement, through the shedding of his blood – to be received by faith. He did this to demonstrate his righteousness, because in his forbearance he had left the sins committed beforehand unpunished.[110]

This is where our always failing and unknowing words reach their highest earthly ascent. Monotheism is grounded in the totalizing awe-driven incomprehensibility of the *existence* of a divine Being Who is Love, and the total incomprehensibility that this Being *might not exist*, live as one in the memory of the lover. It is as inconceivable that Being becomes a Who which exists *for us* as much as it is inconceivable that it does not. Our knowledge seeks always to infinitize, to hold the infinitesimal and the grand, *to be* the gatekeeper of every nuance that can possibly fulfil what is beyond us. We see this astonishing promise of Paradise, as resting on the unification of once impossible tensions, in 2 Corinthians:

> For we know that if the tent that is our earthly home is destroyed, we have a building from God, a house not made with hands, eternal in the heavens. For in this tent we groan, longing to put on our heavenly dwelling, if indeed by putting it on[a] we may not be found naked. For while we are still in this tent, we groan, being burdened – not that we would be unclothed, but that we would be further clothed, so that what is mortal may be swallowed up by life. He who has prepared us for this very thing is God, who has given us the Spirit as a guarantee.[111]

Human life has always lived in the impossible and unknowing territory of that which cannot be undone, and that which is beyond us. Paradise is always before us, and after us, in our midst as we walk, and into us in the grave, growing into our flesh and taking away its shape, ever eliding and eluding our grasp. Our beings yearn for Paradise because Heaven as the infinite memorial Act already became us in the immemorial love which existed "before the foundation of the world."[112] Our knowledge has the appetite for the Transcendent, but we cannot be all these things – this is the core polarity and drama of a human life. Christ as Paradise is the apex in which we extinguish and resurrect all life and hope within us. Christ as singular revelatory figure of monotheism's terminating reality of Paradise is the altar at which we stumble, attempting to make ourselves an offering for the other and needing to receive infinitely more than we are in return. All of creation and the uncreated are bound in Christ whose Being became Sacrifice itself, offering us

---

[109] 1 John 4:10: "Love consists in this: not that we loved God, but that he loved us and sent his Son to be the atoning sacrifice for our sins."
[110] Rev. 3:25   [111] 2 Cor 5:1–5.   [112] 1Pt. 1:20, Eph. 1:4.

the path to Paradise that is more than scratching against fantasy and emptiness, infinitely more than those partial Resurrections of beauty that cannot complete. Within the wounds of Christ, we reveal the one Word Who can offer and receive Paradise as salvific and everlasting; *finally* we encounter the great expiation as the way, the truth, and the life:

> Let not your heart be troubled: ye believe in God, believe also in me. In my Father's house are many mansions: if it were not so, I would have told you. I go to prepare a place for you. And if I go and prepare a place for you, I will come again, and receive you unto myself; that where I am, there ye may be also. And whither I go ye know, and the way ye know. Thomas saith unto him, Lord, we know not whither thou goest; and how can we know the way? Jesus saith unto him, I am the way, the truth, and the life: no man cometh unto the Father, but by me.[113]

Plato's struggle with *lysis* is realized dramatically in Didymus' need to touch Christ's wounds. Christian Monotheism's power comes from the relationship of corrupting body and immortal soul, astonishingly fulfilled in Christ as the body politique – as mystical body who begins in Heaven and is fulfilled in the Paradisal state. We make Home in Christ's flesh Who first offers Himself to us in His Home as His flesh and blood. We breathe in the fragrance of His Word, hear His Call necessitating our entire bodies turn toward Him, touch His garment, see the unseen with the eyes of faith, and taste the sacrifice which alone satisfies all hunger. Our flesh permeates our soul, a reality glorified in Our Lord's agony on Golgotha. And it is illuminated even further in the ecstasy wherein Didymus places his fingers in Christ's wounds touching the spiritual crucible which clarifies the mystery of our bodies transubstantiated through faith and grace.[114] What failed for Plato – the body and temporality – becomes the passageway for transcendence, what could not add up becomes the way beyond the good and perfect *polis*, to Paradise itself. Christian monotheism's historical movement raises to the absolute singular where audaciously the wounds are transformed into perfection:

> A special comeliness will appear in the places scarred by the wounds ... Although those openings of the wounds break the continuity of the tissue, still the greater beauty of glory compensates for all this, so that the body is not less entire, but more perfected ... Christ willed the scars of His wounds to remain on

---

[113] Jn 14:1–6.

[114] Cf. Jn 20:25–29: "'Unless I see the nail marks in his hands and put my finger where the nails were, and put my hand into his side, I will not believe' ... 'Put your finger here; see my hands. Reach out your hand and put it into my side. Stop doubting and believe.' Thomas said to him, 'My Lord and my God!' Then Jesus told him, 'Because you have seen me, you have believed; blessed are those who have not seen and yet have believed'."

> His body, not only to confirm the faith of His disciples, but for other reasons
> also. From these it seems that those scars will always remain on His body.[115]

The hope of our Paradisal bodies dramatically unveils Christ radically uniting
within us, so that each is to become the carrier of the existential polarities which
characterize human life. The nails and thorns which scar Christ pour forth His
essence and fill the Word within us. This radical promise of Christian monotheism means that our scars, the wrinkles on our faces, the aged hands, all the signs
of death, disease, decay, old age, simultaneously evoke perfection – that time
survives inside the orbit of eternity, as death can bring life, and free will, unlike
Oedipus, does not compete with fate. Monotheism offers a Paradise where, with
Christ, we too rise with our scars, but perfuses them with Truth, Goodness,
Beauty and Being. This donative self-emptying communicates the greater glory
of the absolute singular now Incarnated. Plato's sought after universal is now
discovered in the particular, where eternity is realized in flesh and blood, where
our dying bodies reveal the magnificent hope of Paradise. Through Christ, death
is not opposed to Paradise, but the tensions become wholly united. In Christian
monotheism, Paradise is written into our bodies through Christ's incarnation,
death, and resurrection. What is revealed through our bodies in Paradise is not
something lesser, but rather finally we experience the beyondness of reality we
have always sensed – as the Pre-Socrates, the Hymn of Zeus, Oedipus, and Plato
all sensed – but could not quite articulate, could not see commingled within our
flesh. Every philosophical insight we began and could never finish, every tragic
act hinting at transcendence is now grafted to the precarity of human flesh
achieving an impossible perfection – this the powerhouse promise of Paradise in
Christian monotheism.

> Christ is the first-born of God and ... he is the Word of whom all human
> beings have a share. Those who lived according to reason are Christians, even
> though they were classed as atheists, for example, among Greeks, Socrates
> and Heraclitus.[116]

Christian Paradise is not discoverable by inoculating ourselves against death.
It is in the breaking up of the body, in its rupture with time and age that we make
room for Heaven. Our glorified bodies should love the holy death in our living
beings that is Christ's immortalizing armor of flesh and blood, seen in His scars,
filling our bodies with immortalizing perfume:

> In the Messiah, in Christ, God leads us from place to place in one perpetual
> victory parade. Through us, he brings knowledge of Christ. Everywhere we
> go, people breathe in the exquisite fragrance. Because of Christ, we give off

---

[115] Cf. ST III, 54, 4, ad.1–3.   [116] St. Justin Martyr, *First Apology*, 46.

a sweet scent rising to God, which is recognized by those on the way of Salvation – an aroma redolent with life. But those on the way to destruction treat us more like the stench from a rotting corpse.[117]

Monotheism's Paradise cannot occur unless a figure in existence for all existence bears the weight of all the civilizational contradictory powers and bears them befitting human nature. Christ as Expiator is *the* ultimate Atlas who never shrugged.

---

[117] 2 Cor. 14–16.

Bibliography

Aeschylus, *Agamemnon*, in *The Greek Plays: Sixteen Plays by Aeschylus, Sophocles, and Euripides*. Edited by Mary Lefkowitz and James Romm. New York: Modern Library, 2017. 174–79.

Eumenides, in *The Greek Plays: Sixteen Plays by Aeschylus, Sophocles, and Euripides*. Edited by Mary Lefkowitz and James Romm. New York: Modern Library, 2017. 517.

Libation Bearers, in *The Greek Plays: Sixteen Plays by Aeschylus, Sophocles, and Euripides*. Edited by Mary Lefkowitz and James Romm. New York: Modern Library, 2017. 420–23.

Aeschylus, Sophocles, and Euripides. *The Greek Plays: Sixteen Plays by Aeschylus, Sophocles, and Euripides*. Translated by Mary Lefkowitz and James Romm. New York: Modern Library, 2017.

Tragedies and Fragments of Aeschylus, Volumes 1–2. Translated by Edward Hayes Plumptre. Boston: D. C. Heath, 1909. Alighieri, Dante. *The Divine Comedy (the Inferno, the Purgatorio, the Paradiso)*. Translated by John Ciardi. New York: NAL Trade, 2003.

La Vita Nuova. Translated by David Slavitt. Cambridge, MA: Harvard University Press, 2010.

St. Ambrose. *The Letters of St. Ambrose, Bishop of Milan*. Translated by Henry Walford. Oxford: James Parker, 1881.

St. Anselm. *The Devotions of St. Anselm*, edited by Clement Charles Julian Webb. London: Methuen, 1903.

Proslogium, Monologium, Cur Deus Homo, Guanilo's In Behalf of the Fool. Translated by Sidney Norton Deane. Lasalle: Open Court, 1962.

Ante-Nicene Fathers, Volume 9, edited by A. Cleveland Cloxe and Allan Menzies. Buffalo: Christian Literature, 1896. https://books.google.com/books?id=ApMsAAAAYAAJ&printsec=frontcover&source=gbs_ge_summary_r&cad=0#v=onepage&q&f=false.

Aristotle. *The Basic Works of Aristotle*, edited by Richard McKeon. New York: Random House, 1941.

St. Augustine. *Against the Academicians and the Teacher*. Translated by Peter King. Indianapolis: Hackett, 1994.

Augustine Day by Day, edited by John Rotelle. Totowa: Catholic Book, 1986.

Augustine: On the Free Choice of the Will, on Grace and Free Choice, and Other Writings, edited by Peter King. Cambridge: Cambridge University Press, 2010.

City of God, edited by Vernon Bourke. New York: Image, 1958.

Confessions. Translated by Henry Chadwick. New York: Oxford University Press, 1998.

Day by Day with Augustine, edited by Donald X. Burt. Collegeville: Liturgical, 2006.

On Free Choice of the Will. Translated by Thomas Williams. Indianapolis: Hackett, 1993.

Of the Morals of the Catholic Church and on the Morals of the Manicheans. Translated by Richard Stothert. London: Aeterna, 2014.

Nicene and Post-Nicene Fathers: First Series, Volume III, St. Augustine: On the Holy Trinity, Doctrinal Treatises, Moral Treatises, edited by Philip Schaff. New York: Cosimo Classics, 2007.

The Works of Saint Augustine: A Translation for the 21st Century. New York: New City, 2004.

Aristotle, *Nicomachean Ethics*, in *The Basic Works*. Edited by Richard McKeon. New York: Modern Library, 2001. 1177b27–1178a10.

Baird. Forrest, E. *Philosophic Classics: Ancient Philosophy, Volume I*. New York: Routledge, 2010.

Balthasar, Hans Urs von. *The Christian and Anxiety*. San Francisco: Ignatius, 2000.

The Christian State of Life. San Francisco: Ignatius, 2002.

Dare We Hope That All Men Be Saved?: With a Short Discourse on Hell. San Francisco: Ignatius, 2014.

The Glory of the Lord: A Theological Aesthetics, Volume 4: The Realm of Metaphysics in Antiquity. San Francisco: Ignatius, 1989.

Love Alone Is Credible. Translated by David Christopher Schindler. San Francisco: Ignatius, 2004.

A Theology of History. San Francisco: Ignatius, 1994.

Theo-Logic II: Truth of God. San Francisco: Ignatius, 1994.

You Crown the Year with Your Goodness. San Francisco: Ignatius Press, 1989.

St. Bernard of Clairvaux. *On Grace and Free Choice*. Translated by Daniel O'Donovan. Kalamazoo: Cistercian, 1988.

Selected Works. Translated by Gillian Rosemary Evans. New York: Paulist Press, 1987.

Boethius, *Consolatio Philosophiae*, edited by James J. O'Donnell. Bryn Mawr: Bryn Mawr College, 1990.

Book of Common Prayer (1662): International Edition. Westmont: IVP Academic, 2021.

Bernard of Clairvaux. *Selected Works*. Translated by Gillian Rosemary Evans. New York: Paulist Press, 1987.

Breton, Stanislas. *The Word and the Cross*. Translated by Jacquelyn Porter. New York: Fordham University Press, 2002.

Caputo, John D. *Heidegger and Aquinas*. Bronx: Fordham University Press, 1982.

    Religion with/out Religion: The Prayers and Tears of John D. Caputo, edited by James H. Olthuis. New York: Routledge, 2002.

    The Weakness of God: A Theology of the Event. Bloomington: Indiana University Press, 2006.

Chesterton, Gilbert Keith. *All Things Considered*. New York: John Lane, 1916.

    The Collected Works of G.K. Chesterton, Volume 1: Heretics, Orthodoxy, the Blatchford Controversies. San Francisco: Ignatius, 1986.

    The Everlasting Man. San Francisco: Ignatius, 1993.

    Illustrated London News, January 14, 1911.

    "Jesus or Christ," *The Hibbert Journal* 12 (1909) 746–58.

Caputo, John and Gianni Vattimo. *After the Death of God*. New York: Columbia University Press, 2009.

Chrétien, Jean-Louis. *The Ark of Speech*. Translated by Andrew Brown. New York: Routledge, 2004.

    The Unforgettable and the Unhoped For. Translated by Jeffrey Bloechl. New York: Fordham University Press, 2002.

Cioran, Emil. *The Trouble with Being Born*. Translated by Richard Howard. New York: Arcade Press, 2013.

Clarke, William Norris. *Explorations in Metaphysics: Being, God, Person*. South Bend: University of Notre Dame Press, 1995.

    "The Limitation of Act by Potency: Aristotelianism or Neoplatonism." *The New Scholasticism* 26 (1952) 167–94.

    The One and the Many: A Contemporary Thomistic Metaphysics. Notre Dame: University of Notre Dame Press, 2001.

St. Clement of Alexandria, *The Stromata, or Miscellanies*. Mishawaka: Aeterna, 2016.

Davie, Donald, ed. *The New Oxford Book of Christian Verse*. Oxford: Oxford University Press, 1981.

Debout, Jacques. *My Sins of Omission*. Translated by John Francis Scanlan. London: Sands, 1930.

De Lubac, Henri. *Catholicism: Christ and the Common Destiny of Man*. Translated by Lancelot C. Sheppard and Elizabeth Englund. San Francisco: Ignatius, 1988.

    The Drama of Atheistic Humanism. Translated by Mark Sebanc. San Francisco: Ignatius, 1995.

Theology in History. Translated by Anne Englund Nash. San Francisco: Ignatius, 1996.

Derrida, Jacques. *The Gift of Death.* Translated by David Wills. Chicago: University of Chicago Press, 1995.

Desmond, William. *Ethics and the between.* Albany: State University of New York Press, 2001.

The Intimate Strangeness of Being: Metaphysics after Dialectic. Washington, DC: Catholic University of America Press, 2012.

Bible. *The Douay-Rheims New Testament of Our Lord and Savior Jesus Christ.* Compiled by Rev. George Leo Haydock. Monrovia: Catholic Treasures, 1991.

Bible. *The Douay-Rheims Old Testament of the Holy Catholic Bible.* Compiled by Rev. George Leo Haydock. Monrovia: Catholic Treasures, 1992.

Early Greek Philosophy. Translated by Jonathan Barnes. New York: Penguin, 2002.

Eliade, Mircea. *The Myth of the Eternal Return: Cosmos and History.* Princeton: Princeton University Press, 2005.

The Sacred and the Profane: The Nature of Religion. Translated by Willard R. Trask. New York: Harcourt, 1959.

Eliot, Thomas Stearns. *Christianity and Culture.* London: Harvest, 1967.

Gilson, Caitlin Smith. *As It Is in Heaven: Some Christian Questions on the Nature of Paradise.* Eugene: Cascade, 2022.

Immediacy and Meaning: J.K. Huysmans and the Immemorial Origin of Metaphysics. New York: Bloomsbury, 2018.

Metaphysical Presuppositions of Being-in-the-World: A Confrontation Between St. Thomas Aquinas and Martin Heidegger. New York: Continuum, 2010.

The Philosophical Question of Christ. New York: Bloomsbury, 2014.

The Political Dialogue of Nature and Grace: Toward a Phenomenology of Chaste Anarchism. New York: Bloomsbury, 2015.

Subordinated Ethics: Natural Law and Moral Miscellany in Aquinas and Dostoyevsky. Eugene: Cascade, 2020.

Gilson, Étienne. *Being and Some Philosophers.* Toronto: Pontifical Institute of Mediaeval Studies, 1952.

God and Philosophy. New Haven: Yale University Press, 1941.

The Spirit of Mediaeval Philosophy. Translated by Alfred Howard Campbell Downes. New York: Charles Scribner, 1940.

The Spirit of Thomism. New York: Harper, 1964.

The Unity of Philosophical Experience. San Francisco: Ignatius, 1999.

Girard, René. *The One by Whom Scandal Comes.* Translated by Alfred Howard Campbell Downes. East Lansing: Michigan State University Press, 2014.

The Scapegoat. Translated by Yvonne Freccero. Baltimore: Johns Hopkins University, 1986.

Things Hidden since the Foundation of the World. Translated by Stephen Bann and Michael Metteer. Stanford: Stanford University Press, 1987.

Violence and the Sacred. Translated by Patrick Gregory. Baltimore: Johns Hopkins University, 1979.

I See Satan Fall like Lightning. Translated by James G. Williams. Maryknoll, NY: Orbis, 2001.

Hart, David Bentley. *The Hidden and the Manifest: Essays in Theology and Metaphysics*. Grand Rapids: Eerdmans, 2017.

Heidegger, Martin. *Early Greek Thinking*. Translated by David Farrell Krell and Frank A. Capuzzi. New York: Harper and Row, 1975.

The End of Philosophy. Translated by Joan Stambaugh. New York: Harper and Row, 1973.

Phenomenological Interpretations of Aristotle. Translated by Richard Rojcewicz. Bloomington: Indiana University Press, 2001.

Plato's Doctrine of Truth in Philosophy in the Twentieth Century, edited by Henry D. Aiken and William Barrett. New York: Random House, 1962.

Heraclitus, *Heraclitus: The Cosmic Fragments*. Translated by Geoffrey Stephen Kirk. Cambridge: Cambridge University Press, 1954.

Holman, Thomas. "Mythos and History: A Review of Matthew Boulter's 'Repetition and Mythos: Ratzinger's Bonaventure and the Meaning of History'." *Voegelinview*. 01/08/2023.

Jaeger, Werner. *Theology of the Early Greek Philosophers*. New York: Oxford University Press, 1947.

Jaffa, Harry Victor. *Thomism and Aristotelianism*. Chicago: University of Chicago Press, 1952.

Jaspers, Karl. "The Tragic: Awareness, Characteristics, Interpretations," *Tragedy: Modern Essays in Criticism*, edited by Laurence Michel and Richard B. Sewall. Englewood Cliffs: Prentice-Hall, 1963.

St. Justin Martyr. *The Apologies of Justin Martyr*. New York: Harper, 1877.

St. Justin Martyr: The First and Second Apologies. Translated by Leslie William Barnard. Westminster, MD: The Newman Press, 1997.

Kirk, G. S., Raven, Joh Earle and Schofield, Malcolm eds. *The Presocratic Philosophers*. New York: Cambridge University Press, 1983.

Kreeft, Peter. *Everything You Wanted to Know about Heaven but Never Dreamed of Asking*. San Francisco: Ignatius, 1990.

Lattimore, Richard. *The Proper Study: Essays on Western Classics*. New York: St. Martin's, 1962.

Leahy, David G. *Faith and Philosophy*. New York: Ashgate, 2003.

Novitas Mundi. New York: New York University Press, 1980.

Levinas, Emmanuel. *Emmanuel Levinas: Basic Philosophical Writings*, edited by Adriaan T. Peperzak, Simon Critchley and Robert Bernasconi. Bloomington: Indiana University Press, 1996.

The Levinas Reader, edited by Sean Hand. Oxford: Blackwell, 1989.

Totality and Infinity: An Essay on Exteriority. Translated by Alphonso Lingis. Dordrecht: Kluwer, 1991.

Lewis, Clive Staples. *C. S. Lewis Signature Classics: Mere Christianity, the Screwtape Letters, a Grief Observed, the Problem of Pain, Miracles, and the Great Divorce*. New York: Harper, 2001.

A Grief Observed. New York: Harper, 2001.

Till We Have Faces: A Myth Retold. New York: Harper, 1984.

Marion, Jean Luc. *God without Being*. Chicago: University of Chicago Press, 1995.

Maritain, Jacques. *Approaches to God*. Translated by Peter O'Reilly. New York: Harper, 1954.

The Grace and Humanity of Jesus Christ. Translated by Joseph W. Evans. New York: Herder and Herder, 1969.

St. Thomas and the Problem of Evil. Milwaukee: Marquette University Press, 2009.

Mauriac, Francois. *The Inner Presence: Recollection of My Spiritual Life*. Indianapolis: Bobbs-Merrill, 1968.

Milton, John. *Paradise Lost*, edited by Roy C. Flannagan. New York: Dover, 2005.

Newsome Martin, Jennifer. "The Christian Future of Metaphysics: The Carnal Turn in Catholic Theology," *The Future of Christian Metaphysics Conference*. Maynooth: Unpublished lecture, April 2021.

Nietzsche, Friedrich. *The Antichrist*. Translated by Henry Louis Mencken. New York: Alfred A. Knopf, 1918.

Basic Writings. Translated by Walter Kaufmann. New York: Modern Library, 2000.

Beyond Good and Evil: Prelude to a Philosophy of the Future. Translated by Helen Zimmern. New York: Macmillan, 1907.

The Birth of Tragedy: Or Hellenism and Pessimism. Translated by William A. Haussmann. Edinburgh: T. N. Foulis, 1910.

The Essential Nietzsche: Beyond Good and Evil and the Genealogy of Morals. New York: Quarto, 2017.

Human, All Too Human. Translated by Reginald John Hollingdale. Cambridge: Cambridge University Press, 1986.

Philosophy in the Tragic Age of the Greeks. Translated by Marianne Cowan. Washington, DC: Regnery, 1998.

Thus Spoke Zarathustra. Translated by Walter Kaufmann. New York: Random House, 1995.

Twilight of the Idols and the Anti-Christ: Or How to Philosophize with a Hammer. Translated by Reginald John Hollingdale. New York: Penguin, 1990.

The Will to Power. Translated by Walter Kaufmann and Reginald John Hollingdale. New York: Random House, 1967.

O'Regan, Cyril. *The Anatomy of Misremembering*. New York: Herder, 2014.

Theology and the Spaces Apocalyptic. Milwaukee: Marquette University Press, 2009.

O'Rourke, Fran. *Pseudo-Dionysius and the Metaphysics of Aquinas*. South Bend: University of Notre Dame Press, 2005.

Owens, Joseph. *The Doctrine of Being in the Aristotelian Metaphysics*. Toronto: Pontifical Institute of Mediaeval Studies, 1951.

"A Note on Aristotle, De Anima 3.4, 429b9." *Phoenix* 30, 2 (1976) 107–18.

St. Thomas Aquinas on the Existence of God. Albany: State University of New York Press, 1980.

St. Thomas and the Future of Metaphysics. Milwaukee: Marquette University Press, 1957.

Parmenides. *Parmenides of Elea: A Text and Translation*, edited by David Gallop. Ontario: University of Toronto Press, 1984.

Pegis, Anton Charles. *At the Origins of the Thomistic Notion of Man*. New York: Macmillan, 1963.

The Problem of the Soul in the 13th Century. Toronto: Pontifical Institute of Mediaeval Studies, 1934.

St. Thomas and the Greeks. Milwaukee: Marquette University Press, 1939.

"St. Thomas and the Meaning of Human Existence." *Calgary Aquinas Studies*, edited by Anthony Parel, 49–64. Toronto: Pontifical Institute of Mediaeval Studies, 1978.

Peters, Francis E. *Greek Philosophical Terms, a Historical Lexicon*. New York: New York University Press, 1967.

Pieper, Josef. *Death and Immortality*. Translated by Richard Winston and Clara Winston. South Bend: St. Augustine, 2000.

Plato. *The Collected Dialogues of Plato Including the Letters*, edited by Edith Hamilton and Huntington Cairns. New York: Pantheon, 1961.

Plato: Complete Works, edited by John M. Cooper. Indianapolis: Hackett, 1997.

Pope Benedict XVI. *Deus Caritas Est*. Vatican City: Libreria Editrice Vaticana, 2005.

Prtizl, Kurt. "On the Way to Wisdom in Heraclitus." *Phoenix* 39, 4 (1985) 303–16.

Ratzinger, Joseph. *Eschatology: Death and Eternal Life*. Washington, DC: The Catholic University of America Press, 2007.

Rosen, Stanley. *Plato's Symposium*. New Haven: Yale University Press, 1997.

Santayana, George. *The Idea of Christ in the Gospels: Or God in Man, a Critical Essay*. New York: Charles Scribner, 1946.

Sartre, Jean Paul. *Being and Nothingness*. Translated by Hazel E. Barnes. New York: Washington Square, 1993.

  Existentialism Is a Humanism. Translated by Carol Macomber. New Haven: Yale University Press, 2007.

Schindler, David Christopher. *Plato's Critique of Impure Reason: On Goodness and Truth in the Republic*. Washington, DC: The Catholic University of America Press, 2008.

Shestov, Lev. *All Things Are Possible (Apotheosis of Groundlessness)*. Translated by Samuel Solomonovitch Kotelianksy. New York: Robert McBride, 1920.

  Athens and Jerusalem. Translated by Bernard Martin. Athens: Ohio University Press, 1966.

Sophocles. *The Complete Greek Tragedies, Volume 2: Sophocles*, edited by David Grene and Richmond Lattimore. Chicago: University of Chicago Press, 1992.

  The Three Theban Plays. Translated by Robert Fagles. New York: Penguin, 1984.

Taylor, Alfred Edward. *Plato: The Man and His Works*. London: Methuen, 1927.

  Plato. New York: New York University Press, 1926.

  The "Parmenides" of Plato. New York: Oxford University Press, 1934.

Tertullian. *Treatise on the Incarnation De Carne Christi*, edited by Ernest Evans. London: Society for Promoting Christian Knowledge, 1956.

St. Thomas Aquinas. *On Being and Essence (De Ente et Essentia)*. Translated by Armand Maurer. Toronto: Pontifical Institute of Mediaeval Studies, 1949.

  Commentary on Aristotle's Politics. Translated by Richard J. Regan. Indianapolis: Hackett, 2007.

  Commentary on the De Anima. Translated by Kenelm Foster and Silvester Humphries. New Haven: Yale University Press, 1951.

  Commentary on the Metaphysics. Translated by John P. Rowen. South Bend: Dumb Ox, 1995.

  Commentary on the Sentences. Translated by Beth Mortensen. Steubenville: Emmaus, 2017.

  In Librum Beati Dionysii de Divinis Nominibus Expositio, edited by Ceslai Pera and Caroli Mazzantini. Turin: Marietti, 1950.

  Quaestiones Disputatae de Potentia. Translated by the English Dominican Fathers. Westminster: Newman, 1952.

Summa Theologiae, edited by Thomas Gilby. New York: Cambridge University Press, 1967.

Summa Contra Gentiles. Translated by James F. Anderson. South Bend: University of Notre Dame Press, 1992.

De Veritate. Translated by Robert W. Mulligan. Chicago: Henry Regnery, 1952.

Sophocles, *Antigone*, in *The Greek Plays: Sixteen Plays by Aeschylus, Sophocles, and Euripides*. Edited by Mary Lefkowitz and James Romm. New York: Modern Library, 2017. 940–43.

Oedipus Rex, in *The Greek Plays: Sixteen Plays by Aeschylus, Sophocles, and Euripides*. Edited by Mary Lefkowitz and James Romm. New York: Modern Library, 2017. 1205–16.

Tillich, Paul. *Systematic Theology, Volume* I. Chicago: The University of Chicago Press, 1951.

Unamuno, Miguel. *Tragic Sense of Life*. Translated by John Ernest Crawford Flitch, Mineola: Dover, 1952.

Vattimo, Gianni, and Pier Aldo Rovatti, eds. *Weak Thought*. Albany: State University of New York Press, 2012.

Velasquez, Manuel. *Philosophy: A Text with Readings, 11th Ed.* Boston: Cengage, 2010.

Voegelin, Eric. *Order and History Volume 1: Israel and Revelation (Collected Works of Eric Voegelin, Volume 14)*, edited by Maurice P. Hogan. Columbia: University of Missouri Press, 2001.

Order and History Volume 2: The World of the Polis (Collected Works of Eric Voegelin, Volume 15), edited by Athanasios Moulakis. Columbia: University of Missouri Press, 2000.

Order and History Volume 3: Plato and Aristotle (Collected Works of Eric Voegelin, Volume 16), edited By Dante Germino. Columbia: University of Missouri Press, 1999.

Order and History Volume 4: The Ecumenic Age. Baton Rouge: Louisiana State University Press, 1974.

What Is History? And Other Late Unpublished Writings (Collected Works Volume 28), edited by Thomas A. Hollweck and Paul Caringella. Columbia: University of Missouri Press, 1990.

Walsh, David. *Guarded by Mystery Meaning in a Postmodern Age*. Washington, DC: Catholic University of America Press, 1999.

Wolfe, Christopher James. "Plato's and Aristotle's Answers to the Parmenides Problem." Review of Metaphysics 65, 2 (June, 2012) 747–64.

Xenophanes, fr. 6 in Forrest Baird. *Philosophic Classics: Ancient Philosophy*, Volume I. New York: Routledge, 2010. 18.

Acknowledgments

Very grateful to my dear friend, the artist Carol Scott (Professor Emeritus of Art, University of Holy Cross), for her generous permission to use her exceptional and fitting art, which will enhance the experience for the reader. Many thanks to Drs. Paul Moser and Chad Meister for their keen guidance in the process. Immensely grateful to Vidya Ashwin Krishnan for her editorial acumen and generous assistance.

To my family, Fred, Mary, and Lily, for their cherished support and love.

Cambridge Elements ☰

Religion and Monotheism

Paul K. Moser

Loyola University Chicago

Paul K. Moser is Professor of Philosophy at Loyola University Chicago. He is the author of *God in Moral Experience; Paul's Gospel of Divine Self-Sacrifice; The Divine Goodness of Jesus; Divine Guidance; Understanding Religious Experience; The God Relationship; The Elusive God* (winner of national book award from the Jesuit Honor Society); *The Evidence for God; The Severity of God; Knowledge and Evidence* (all Cambridge University Press); and *Philosophy after Objectivity* (Oxford University Press); coauthor of *Theory of Knowledge* (Oxford University Press); editor of *Jesus and Philosophy* (Cambridge University Press) and *The Oxford Handbook of Epistemology* (Oxford University Press); and coeditor of *The Wisdom of the Christian Faith* (Cambridge University Press). He is the coeditor with Chad Meister of the book series *Cambridge Studies in Religion, Philosophy, and Society.*

Chad Meister

Affiliate Scholar, Ansari Institute for Global Engagement with Religion, University of Notre Dame

Chad Meister is Affiliate Scholar at the Ansari Institute for Global Engagement with Religion at the University of Notre Dame. His authored and co-authored books include *Evil: A Guide for the Perplexed* (Bloomsbury Academic, 2nd edition); *Introducing Philosophy of Religion* (Routledge); *Introducing Christian Thought* (Routledge, 2nd edition); and *Contemporary Philosophical Theology* (Routledge). He has edited or co-edited the following: *The Oxford Handbook of Religious Diversity* (Oxford University Press); *Debating Christian Theism* (Oxford University Press); with Paul Moser, *The Cambridge Companion to the Problem of Evil* (Cambridge University Press); and with Charles Taliaferro, *The History of Evil* (Routledge, in six volumes). He is the co-editor with Paul Moser of the book series *Cambridge Studies in Religion, Philosophy, and Society.*

About the Series

This Cambridge Element series publishes original concise volumes on monotheism and its significance. Monotheism has occupied inquirers since the time of the Biblical patriarch, and it continues to attract interdisciplinary academic work today. Engaging, current, and concise, the Elements benefit teachers, researched, and advanced students in religious studies, Biblical studies, theology, philosophy of religion, and related fields.

Cambridge Elements ≡

Religion and Monotheism

Elements in the Series

A full series listing is available at: www.cambridge.org/er&m

Printed in the United States
by Baker & Taylor Publisher Services